Weapons of World War II (Artillery)

CONTENTS

4-5 Introduction
6-7 Artillery in World War Two
8 Field Guns
9 M1 155mm Long Tom
10 M1 (8-inch) 203mm
11 M1 4.5-inch
12 Feld Kanone 16 nA
13 100mm K17
14 100mm sK18
15 150mm & 170mm K18
16 M1931/37 122mm
17 M1944 100mm
18 M1939 Divisional Gun 76mm USV
19 M1942 Divisional Gun 76mm ZiS-3
20 Type 90 75mm
21 Type 92 100mm
22 Canon de 75 Modele 1897
23 Canon de 105L Mle 1936 Schneider
24 Canon de 155mm GPF
25 Ordnance QF 18-pounder
26 Ordnance QF 25-pounder
27 BL 4.5-inch & 5.5-inch Medium Guns
28 Ansaldo 149/40 M1935
29 Howitzers
30 M1 Pack 75mm
31 M2 105mm
32 M1 155mm 'Long Tom'
33 M3 Light
34 M1 240mm
35 leFH 18M Light
36 leFH 18/40 Light
37 sFH 18 150mm
38 M1937 & M1938 152mm; M1938 122mm
39 Type 92 Light
40 Canon de 105 Court mle 1934 Schneider
41 BL 7.2-inch

42 QF 4.5-inch
43 Obice M75/18 Modello 34
44 Anti-tank Guns
45 M3 37mm
46 M5 76mm
47 PaK 35/36 37mm & PaK 38 50mm
48 PaK 40 75mm
49 ZiS-2 57mm
50 M42 45mm
51 Type 1 AT Gun 47mm
52 Modele 1937 APX 47mm
53 Ordnance QF 2-pounder & 6-pounder
54 Ordnance QF 17-pounder
55 Hotchkiss 25mm
58 Cannone da 90/53
59 Anti-aircraft Guns
60 M1 Dual Purpose 90mm
61 M1 37mm Gun
62 Flak 18 88mm
63 Flak 38 105mm & Flak 40 128mm
64 Bofors 40mm & Oerlikon 20mm
65 72-K 25mm
66 61-K 37mm
67 Type 3 120mm
68 Ordnance QF 3.7-inch
69 Self-propelled Artillery
70 M7 105mm Priest
71 M40 155mm & M12 155mm
72 sIG 33 PzKpfw I Bison
73 105mm Wespe & 150mm Hummel
74 Sturmgeschutz III
75 SU-76
76 ISU-122 & ISU-152
77 Sexton
78 Bishop
79 Mountain Artillery
80 Gebirgshaubitze 40 105mm
81 M1938 76mm Mountain Gun
82 Type 94 75mm
83 Ordnance QF 3.7-inch Mountain Howitzer
84 Cannone da 65/17
85 Rocket Artillery
86 T-34 Calliope 4.5-inch Multiple Rocket Launcher
87 Nebelwerfer 42 210mm & 300mm
88 Katyusha
89 Z Battery & Land Mattress
90 Railway Artillery
91 Schwerer Gustav
92 K5 283mm

93 K12E 210mm
94 BL 9.2-inch Mk XIII
95 BL 18-inch Howitzer & 13.5-inch Gun
96 Naval, Coastal, Siege Artillery
97 14-inch 45 & 50-calibre
98 16-inch 45 & 50-calibre
99 5-inch 38-calibre Mark 12
100 8-inch 55-calibre Mark 12 & 15
101 6-inch 47-calibre Mark 16
102 M1919 16-inch 50-calibre Coastal Defence Gun
103 BL 14-inch Mk VII
104 BL 15-inch & 16-inch Mk I
105 380mm SK C/34
106 150mm SK C/28
107 203mm SK C/34
108 BL 6-inch Mk XXIII
109 BL 8-inch Mk VIII
110 Type 36 45-calibre 14-inch
111 41/45 3rd Year Type
112 18.1-inch Type 94 Naval Rifle
113 Granatenwerfer 69 210mm
114 Glossary

ABOVE: King George VI and Royal Navy officers tour the battleship HMS *King George V* with its BL 14-inch 50-calibre Mk VII guns. (COLLECTIONS OF THE IMPERIAL WAR MUSEUMS VIA WIKIMEDIA COMMONS)

BELOW LEFT: An Ordnance QF 25-pounder gun, workhorse of the British Army during World War Two, fires at night during the Battle of El Alamein. (COLLECTIONS OF THE IMPERIAL WAR MUSEUMS VIA WIKIMEDIA COMMONS)

BELOW: A gun crew mans a camouflaged 88mm flak gun in a mountainous emplacement in Scandinavia. (CREATIVE COMMONS BUNDESARCHIV BILD VIA WIKIMEDIA COMMONS)

ISBN: 978 1 83632 185 9
Editor: Mike Haskew
Senior editor, specials: Roger Mortimer
Email: roger.mortimer@keypublishing.com
Cover Design: Steve Donovan
Design: SJmagic DESIGN SERVICES, India
Advertising Sales Manager: Sam Clark
Email: sam.clark@keypublishing.com
Tel: 01780 755131
Advertising Production: Becky Antoniades
Email: Rebecca.antoniades@keypublishing.com

SUBSCRIPTION/MAIL ORDER
Key Publishing Ltd, PO Box 300, Stamford, Lincs, PE9 1NA
Tel: 01780 480404
Subscriptions email: subs@keypublishing.com
Mail Order email: orders@keypublishing.com
Website: www.keypublishing.com/shop

PUBLISHING
Group CEO: Adrian Cox
Publisher: Steve O'Hara

Published by
Key Publishing Ltd, PO Box 100, Stamford, Lincs, PE9 1XQ

Tel: 01780 755131
Website: www.keypublishing.com

PRINTING
Precision Colour Printing Ltd, Haldane, Halesfield 1, Telford, Shropshire. TF7 4QQ

DISTRIBUTION
Seymour Distribution Ltd, 2 Poultry Avenue, London, EC1A 9PU
Enquiries Line: 02074 294000.

Artillery Weapons of World War II

Introduction

The artillery of World War Two can trace its heritage to much earlier times. From great clouds of flaming arrows to the catapult that hurled massive boulders toward an earthen or stone rampart, the evolution of artillery has shaped the history of the world.

By the 20th century, the terrible destructive power of artillery had been experienced on an unprecedented scale on the Western Front during World War One. A generation later, artillery reached the apex of its capacity to influence the course of military events. On numerous occasions, timely and accurate artillery fire paved the way for an assault, broke up an enemy attack or softened targets to the point of capitulation. At sea, the big guns roared in the twilight of the battleship, giving way to a new era of modern weaponry that could be considered advances in the awesome art of artillery. World War Two simply would not have progressed as it did without the thunder of the big gun.

While there is evidence that the bow and arrow, catapult and other weapons that may be deemed the earliest forms artillery entered combat in ancient times, the battlefield use of artillery as more

clearly defined in the modern period – the firing of a projectile with the aid of a propellant such as gunpowder – is believed to have its origins in the Chinese Soong Dynasty of the late 12th Century.

In the West, the siege of Algeciras in the 14th Century saw both attacking Christian and defending Muslim forces utilise artillery. The English are said to have deployed artillery at the Battle of Crécy in 1346 during the Hundred Years' War. And through the centuries, evolving weapons systems brought artillery to the fore on the field of conflict. Skilful and concentrated use of fire that must be acknowledged as heavier and therefore more devastating than the weapons wielded and shouldered by infantrymen was swiftly acknowledged for its potential to turn the tide of a battle or military campaign and even weigh heavily on the outcome of an entire war.

While artillery itself might prove decisive, there were early challenges. As guns grew in size and potency, their transportation to and from the field became problematic. Heavier projectiles required refinements in propellant potency, and rates of fire could be ponderously slow. However, none of these factors could diminish the prospective combat prowess of the cannon and its more specialised descendants, the howitzer, siege gun, anti-tank and anti-aircraft weapons, railway guns, self-propelled artillery, rocket-firing weapons and more.

Swedish King Gustavus Adolphus is credited with urging the development of light artillery, including the three-pounder gun used by his troops during the Thirty Years' War of the early 1600s. In 1650, the foremost treatise of the age concerning the use of artillery was written and published by Polish-Lithuanian tactician Casimir Siemienowicz, a contemporary expert on the topic. His *Great Art of Artillery, the First Part*, shaped theory and implementation of such weaponry for the next two centuries and the basic composition of artillery did not substantially change during the period.

With the coming of the Industrial Revolution in the 18th Century, the refinement of artillery began in earnest. The concentration of workers in factories, improvements in metallurgy, the concept of interchangeable parts developed by American inventor Eli Whitney, the introduction of steam power, the emergence of the railroad as a prime mover of heavy weapons and other factors brought artillery to the forefront of warfare. By the era of empire building, wars of succession, revolutionary conflicts and the age of Napoleon Bonaparte, artillery had become an integral part of military strategy and tactics on land, while at sea the warship, with its menacing cannon, dictated the course of events in major naval battles and the exercise of trade and commerce.

From 1850 forward, the development of modern artillery proceeded at an astounding pace, with the introduction

of breechloading and rifled weapons to augment the traditional smoothbore and muzzle-loading types. During the Crimean War, the fabled Charge of the Light Brigade saw British cavalry decimated by a concentration of Russian artillery fire. The battlefields of the American Civil War were littered with the bodies of infantrymen slaughtered in great numbers by field artillery firing case, grapeshot, fragmentation and solid rounds – highly specialised shells intended to inflict maximum casualties. Indeed, artillery was recognised as having the capability to shatter the enemy's advance, bombard its rear areas and influence military movement from over the horizon and out of sight.

Modern warfare is forever marked by the use of artillery and will continue to be for centuries to come. This volume explores the most telling chapter in its history as the sledgehammer that barked and battered its way to immortality during World War Two.

Michael E Haskew

ABOVE: This colourful tapestry depicts Indian troops utilising artillery during the 16th century. (BABURNAMA VIA WIKIMEDIA COMMONS)

LEFT: Union Army cannon decimate a Confederate charge at the Battle of Stones River in the American Civil War. (LIBRARY OF CONGRESS VIA WIKIMEDIA COMMONS)

LEFT: A heavy German railway gun moves into firing position at the Battle of Verdun during World War One. (CREATIVE COMMONS BUNDESARCHIV BILD VIA WIKIMEDIA COMMONS)

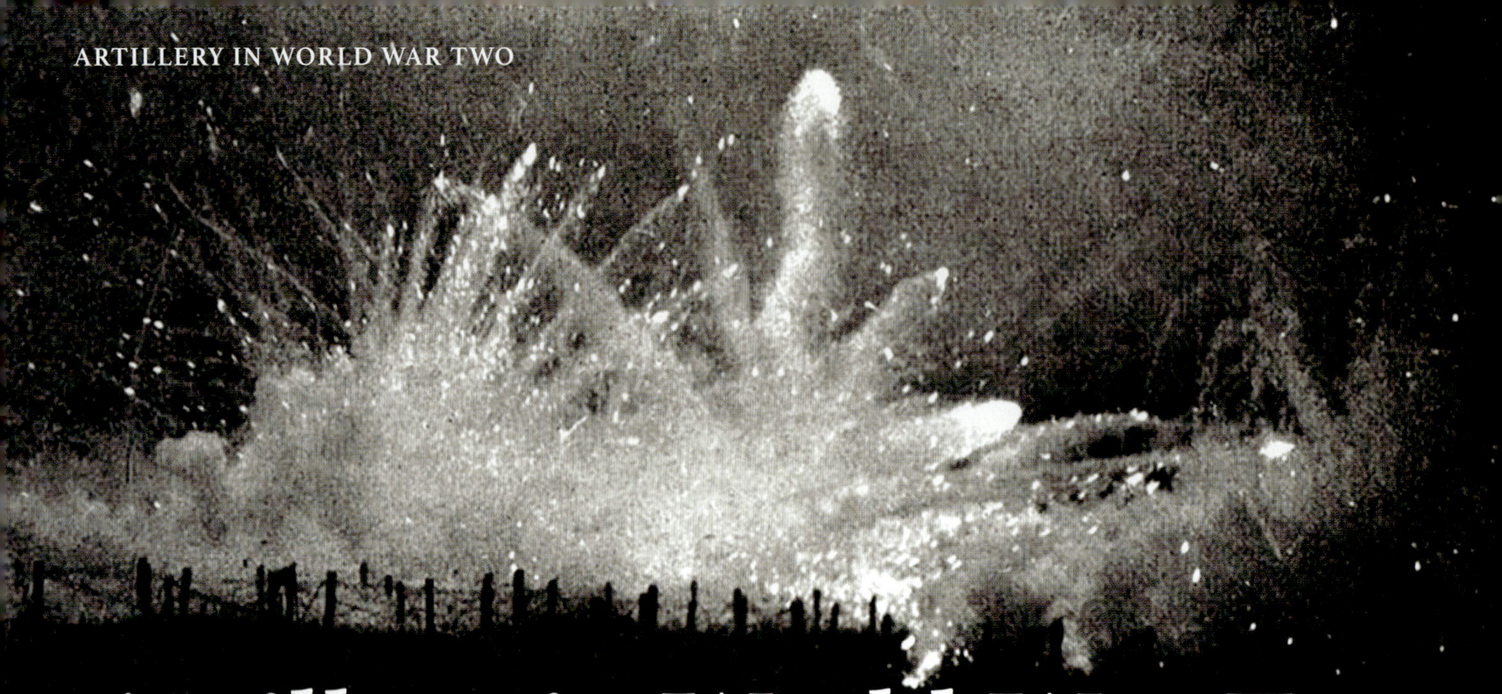

Artillery in World War Two

Tactical Support on the front line

ABOVE: A barrage of German artillery fire erupts along a British trench line near the Belgian town of Ypres during World War One. (COLONEL GEORGE G NAISMITH VIA WIKIPEDIA COMMONS)

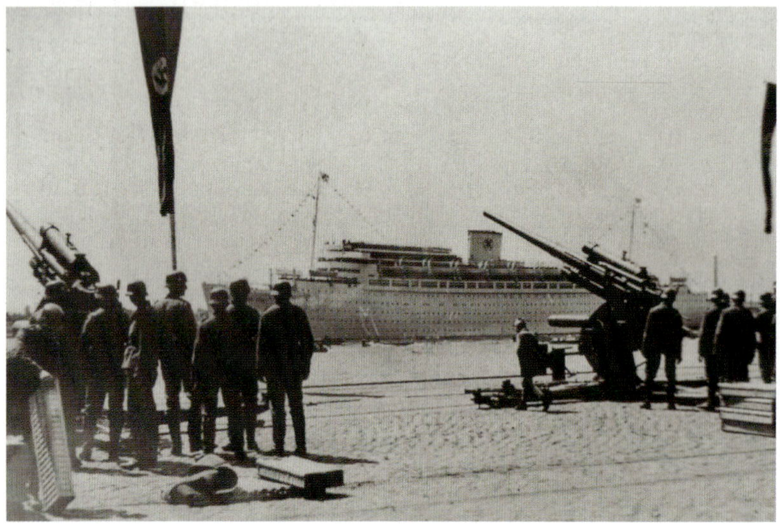

RIGHT: German gun crews stand beside their 88mm weapons and prepare to fire a salute to troops returning from Spain in the 1930s. (CREATIVE COMMONS TORMENTOR4555 VIA WIKIMEDIA COMMONS)

The old saying goes that artillery is the king of the battlefield. This description is derived from its ability to deliver devastating firepower from a relative distance, accurately and in a manner that is often more efficient and less costly than air power.

However, the term also arises from the age old strategic and tactical game of chess. While the infantry is the 'Queen' of the battlefield, with its manoeuvrability and versatile combat disposition, the artillery is called the 'King' because it strikes in any direction with decisive might. While the Queen utilises movement, the king may be limited in is ability to move only a single square on the chessboard, but the result of that movement is telling.

By World War Two, the capability of artillery to shape the modern battlefield was undeniable. The lessons of World War One were to exert substantial influence on military thinking. For example, the use of shrapnel shells had been deemed ineffective against fixed fortifications or trench lines, thus high-explosive shells would become a standard of the future. Specialisation of artillery developed with the airplane and the appearance of the tank in combat – artillery weapons specifically designed to counter them were under development during World War One and the inter-war years, making their presence common by 1939.

Coastal artillery was somewhat de-emphasized as guns were at times removed from their casemates and redesigned for field use. Likewise, fixed fortifications and their relative contribution to defence were re-examined. Although the French government spent millions to construct the sturdy barrier of the Maginot Line, General George S Patton Jr, the controversial American firebrand, declared: "Fixed fortifications are monuments to the stupidity of man." Historians are left

RIGHT: A US Marine surveys the battle-scarred landscape at Bloody Ridge after artillery decimated attacking Japanese soldiers on Guadalcanal. (UNITED STATES GOVERNMENT VIA WIKIMEDIA COMMONS)

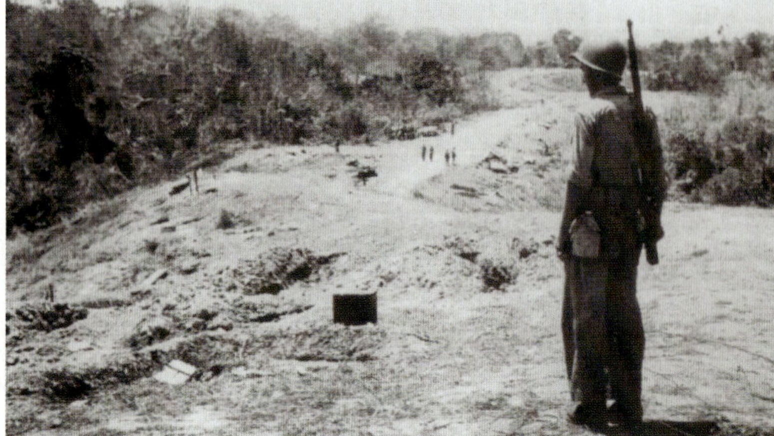

to weigh the defeat of the Maginot Line by the Germans in 1940 and the truth in Patton's words, but it is clear that artillery in fixed and fortified positions may have seen its swan song in the early days of World War Two. Witness further the rapid conquest of Fort Eban-Emael in 1940, its menacing guns considered an impregnable impediment to attack along the Belgian frontier. In just hours, a group intrepid German airborne troops subdued the mighty fortress.

With the outbreak of war, artillery became a hallmark of offensive operations. The Japanese had shown the power of field guns in their campaigns on the Asian continent beginning in 1931 and their victories over Chinese forces through the Second Sino-Japanese War in 1937. The Nazi blitzkrieg was characterised by the use of aircraft, armoured spearheads exploiting breaches in enemy lines and the use of artillery to facilitate those breaches with concentrated fire against prepared positions. When German forces launched Operation Barbarossa, the invasion of the Soviet Union, across a 1,000-mile front on June 22, 1941, they fielded approximately 7,000 guns to open their huge offensive.

In the Pacific, there is no question that American artillery was decisive in ousting the Japanese from the island of Guadalcanal. Vital in the defence of Henderson Field, 800 men of the 1st Marine Raider Battalion, commanded by Colonel Merritt A 'Red Mike' Edson, made a valiant stand against desperate Japanese attacks along a ridgeline on September 12-14, 1942. Ever after, the high ground has been remembered as 'Bloody Ridge' and it was the concentrated fire of the 11th Marine Regiment, their 75mm and 105mm howitzers blasting continually, that helped the defenders hold their vital positions. The 105s had discharged 1,992 shells, while the 75s had contributed more than 1,000, when

the enemy tide receded. Many of the 1,200 Japanese killed and wounded in the assaults resulted from the timely and accurate Marine artillery. One Japanese officer captured in the battle was reported as having asked to see the "automatic artillery" the Marines had employed. Apparently, the enemy had been astonished at the rate of fire.

The famous Ordnance QF 25-pounder was lifted to prominence during the fighting in the Western Desert, and one historian called the prolonged struggle against the Afrika Korps under General Erwin Rommel as being "the finest hour of the 25-pdr." While the fearsome German 88mm anti-aircraft gun became legend when employed in the anti-tank role, the 25-pounder was nearly 88mm itself (actually 3.45in or 87.6mm to be exact) and proved at times to be the only field gun that could take on German tanks in North Africa and consistently prevail. The fighting around Tobruk in the spring of 1942 and the later pivotal battle of El Alamein attest to the 25-pounder's performance. At Stalingrad, a single 76mm anti-tank gun was credited

with destroying an impressive tally – six German tanks, eight armoured cars, and 11 trucks carrying supplies – when a Red Army photographer happened across the crew working feverishly and snapped an image of desperate combat.

Many artillery pieces of World War Two were holdovers from World War One, still effective and available in quantity in the mid-20th Century. The French 75mm gun was deployed in great quantities, with many of them falling into German hands with the capitulation of 1940. These guns were often pressed into service with the Wehrmacht, as were weapons produced at the famed Skoda Works in Czechoslovakia when that country fell under the control of Germany in March 1939, five months before the outbreak of World War Two in Europe.

Stories of artillery in action during World War Two abound. Big guns had already earned their place as pivotal weapons on the modern battlefield, but during the conflict their offensive and defensive capabilities reached new heights.

Field Guns

Close to the Ground Forces

The mention of artillery often conjures up images of the field gun, the quintessential weapon that exhibits mobility, long-range or direct fire support and versatility. The field gun could swiftly impact the course of a battle along the front lines, either deployed in a specific mission against an identified target or in a broader context from greater distance.

The acknowledgment of Allied artillery as a decisive weapon of land warfare was exemplified in an anonymous comment from *The Field Artillery Journal*, which stated:

"Without our artillery we would be swimming in the Channel instead of being in Germany. And I am sure the Germans fear that more than any arm of our army."

The field gun is characterised by its ability to fire and relocate, often constructed with a wheeled carriage and capable of being towed by vehicles. These weapons have regularly been called to fire in support of infantry either as a prelude to attack or in direct repulse of an enemy thrust. The primary role of field artillery is to suppress, destroy or neutralise the enemy. Field guns have been constructed typically to fire on a flatter trajectory than the howitzer, whose angle of fire is at a greater arc. The field gun is a general purpose weapon that developed without a specified role such as coastal or anti-aircraft artillery. However, during the course of World War Two, the field gun evolved into a multi-purpose weapon, both in traditional infantry support but also in the anti-tank role and in reduction of enemy strongpoints.

The infantry gun, a sub-category of the field gun, included smaller and lighter artillery pieces that were often seen close to the front lines and firing in direct support of infantry operations. Infantry guns offered immediate tactical firepower in opposition to enemy entrenchments or mechanised forces that were within sight of the infantry and locked in direct combat. They were designed with the unique demands of close-quarter combat in mind, typically with short barrels and lower muzzle velocity. Amid this rising specialisation, the line between 'gun' and 'howitzer' definitions began to blur, even to the extent that some field artillery pieces were referred to as 'gun-howitzers', capable of firing on a flat trajectory or at a more pronounced plunging angle for better penetration of hard targets.

Field Marshal Bernard Montgomery, hero of El Alamein, summed up the importance of field artillery: "The harder the fighting and the longer the war, the more infantry and, in fact, all the arms, lean on the gunners."

Examples of field artillery pieces and infantry guns that played prominent roles in World War Two include the British 4.5- and 5.5-inch medium guns and 25-pounder, the American 37mm and 155mm Long Tom, the German 105mm leFH 18 and the Soviet ZiS-3. The American workhorse light 105mm M3 is an example of a gun-howitzer.

M1 155mm Long Tom

When the United States entered World War One in 1917, its military was unprepared for such an immense conflict and the commitment of men required weapons and equipment that were not readily available from US sources. Such was the case with heavy field artillery, with the US Army depending largely on the French Canon de 155mm GPF for fire support. After the conflict concluded, the US military establishment convened the Caliber Board, a panel to conduct a comprehensive review of the use of artillery in future conflicts.

Dubbed the Westervelt Board after its chief, Brigadier General William Westervelt, the group shaped the advent of an artillery component that was second to none during World War Two. Among its findings was the need for the army to develop and deploy a 155mm field gun of American origin. The result was the 155mm gun M1, nicknamed 'Long Tom', a moniker that had origins in earlier forms of US heavy weapons. The Long Tom was present on virtually every front where American land forces were deployed

ABOVE: This 155mm Long Tom resides at the Aberdeen Proving Ground US Army Ordnance Museum in Maryland. (CREATIVE COMMONS MARK PELLEGRINI VIA WIKIMEDIA COMMONS)

M1 155mm Long Tom	
Country of Origin	USA
Calibre	155mm
Crew	14
Range	14.7 miles
Rate of Fire	1 round per 90 seconds
Number manufactured	1,882

during World War Two, its range of nearly 15 miles with a high explosive shell weighing 100lb and its accuracy and impact of amazing quality making the weapon a mainstay.

The Long Tom was a heavy weapon at more than 15 tonnes, requiring a prime trasnporter such as the Allis-Chalmers M4 high-speed tractor to move cross country or on roadways. Its employment of the split-trail carriage M1 with all-welded construction provided a quite stable platform to absorb the substantial recoil. The M1 155mm design and testing were concluded in the late 1930s and production began in 1940. Two years later, its first shot in anger was fired by Battery A, 36th Field Artillery, on December 24, 1942, during the North Africa campaign. The original M1 was upgraded to the M1A1 in 1941 with a modified breech ring, while the M2 with additional breech modification was built from 1945.

Throughout World War Two, the Long Tom equipped 33 US Army field artillery battalions at the corps level in theUS table of organisation and equipment during operations in the Mediterranean and Europe. The US Marines notably used the big gun during the fighting in the Solomon Islands of the South Pacific and into the Philippines campaign from 1943 onward.

As the Long Tom became a standard weapon in the US arsenal, its reputation for effectiveness was widely known. Its barrel length was imposing at 22ft, 10in, while its height was nearly nine feet. Shells and propellant were loaded separately into the Asbury mechanism breech. Powder charges were stacked depending on the range to target.

The 155mm M1A1 served well into the 1960s, including deployments during the Korean War and Vietnam. It served as the basis for the M40 self-propelled gun and was redesignated the M59 after World War Two.

BELOW LEFT: Long Tom crews fire their guns from earthen emplacements on the island of Okinawa in 1945. (US ARMY VIA WIKIMEDIA COMMONS)

BELOW: This Long Tom was brought ashore at Nettuno in 1944, shortly after the Anzio landings. (US NATIONAL ARCHIVES AND RECORDS ADMINISTRATION VIA WIKIMEDIA COMMONS)

M1 (8-inch) 203mm

RIGHT: This M1 8-inch 203mm gun is on display at Fort Sill, Oklahoma. (CREATIVE COMMONS STURMVOGEL 66 VIA WIKIMEDIA COMMONS)

The (8-inch) 203mm Gun M1 was the longest range weapon in the US Army field artillery arsenal during World War Two.

The post-World War One Westervelt Board had identified the requirement for a heavy field gun with a bore of eight inches and range of more than 20 miles while hurling a shell that weighed approximately 200lb. Research began on the heavy weapon in the mid-1920s, but made little progress until resumption in 1940 amid other specifications, such as the ability to transport it overland aboard two separate movers, one that would carry the barrel and recoil mechanism and the other the carriage, at an impressive speed of 25mph. Each of the component loads was to weigh no more than 22 tonnes. While sharing a carriage with the M1 240mm howitzer simplified the development process and ammunition that was common with the 8-inch coastal guns of the day and the main armament of the US Navy's heavy cruisers was beneficial, the M1 203mm gun was not approved for general service until 1943.

BELOW: An 8-inch 203mm gun blasts German positions at the French port of Brest. (UNITED KINGDOM GOVERNMENT VIA WIKIMEDIA COMMONS)

BOTTOM: This 8-inch 203mm gun is displayed outdoors at the US Army Ordnance Museum, Aberdeen Proving Ground, Maryland. (CREATIVE COMMONS MARK PELLEGRINI VIA WIKIMEDIA COMMONS)

In practice, the gun exhibited problems, particularly excessive wear on the bore during sustained operations. This led to erosion of accuracy, but the system was the best available at the time as the United States became more deeply committed to land operations during World War Two. Initially transported by the Mack NO 7½-tonne truck and then the chassis of M3 tanks and recovery vehicles and the M6 high-speed tractor, the weapon was assembled for firing with the aid of the M2 truck-mounted crane and could become operational in about two hours. In the absence of the crane, a combination of winches, cables and tractor power could accomplish the task.

The M1 203mm gun equipped five artillery battalions in Italy and France, along with three battalions in the Pacific. Each battalion consisted of six guns organised into three two-gun batteries, and the weapon was primarily employed in a long-range role against enemy bridges, communications centres, troop concentrations and fortifications. It was also notable for exchanges with long-range German artillery. The gun was present during the assaults on Monte Cassino in Italy and the reduction of the masonry fortifications in the Philippine capital of Manila, where the Japanese had taken refuge in the fight for the city.

The M1 203mm weighed more than 69,000lb and was operated with an interrupted screw breech. Like other US field artillery pieces, it was stabilised by the split trail carriage. A few of the guns were placed in service with the British Army.

M1 (8-inch) 203mm Gun	
Country of Origin	USA
Calibre	203mm (8-inch)
Crew	23-25 incl. chief of section & drivers
Range	20.24 miles
Rate of Fire	1 round per minute
Number manufactured	139

M1 4.5-inch

Altered for compatibility with British ammo

The M1 4.5-inch gun was a byproduct of the American experience on the Western Front during World War One. The US Army had deployed the M1906 4.7-inch field gun in limited numbers and, by 1920, the military establishment had determined that a new medium field gun was needed. The Ordnance Department set about developing the new 4.7-inch gun concurrently with the 155mm howitzer, and while the 155mm was designated for deployment at the division level, the 4.7-inch gun was to be a corps weapon. To simplify the progression, these two systems were to share the same carriage.

By 1922, the army endorsed the 4.7-inch M1922E gun on carriage M1921E, but further progress was stymied by a lack of funds and this system never entered production. Nearly 20 years later, the initiative was renewed as World War Two erupted. The bore diameter was altered to 4.5 inches or 114mm to become compatible with British ammunition of the same calibre fired by the BL 4.5-inch medium field gun. As such, the approved 4.7-inch gun T3 became the production model that was fielded during World War Two.

The 4.5-inch gun sported a barrel that was 15ft, 7in long. It weighed 12,465lb and was transported by towing prime movers. The gun utilised an interrupted screw breech and a hydro-pneumatic recoil system supported by the substantial split trail carriage, further braced by a retractable pedestal while in firing position. Targets were acquired via an M12 panoramic sight.

The weapon proved to have exceptional range at more than 14½ miles, but its ammunition was inferior and hindered its effectiveness. The 55-pound high explosive shell was produced from low grade steel, which required thicker shell walls and resulted in an inferior bursting charge, actually delivering a lesser quantity of explosive than the contemporary 105mm high explosive shell.

Although the M1 4.5-inch gun was standardised in the spring of 1941, production didn't start until the autumn of 1942, and the short run ceased by February 1944. The system eventually reached 17 field artillery battalions engaged in western Europe

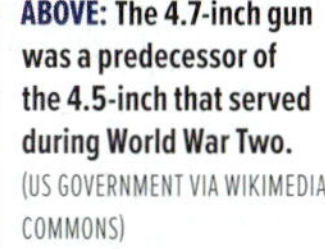

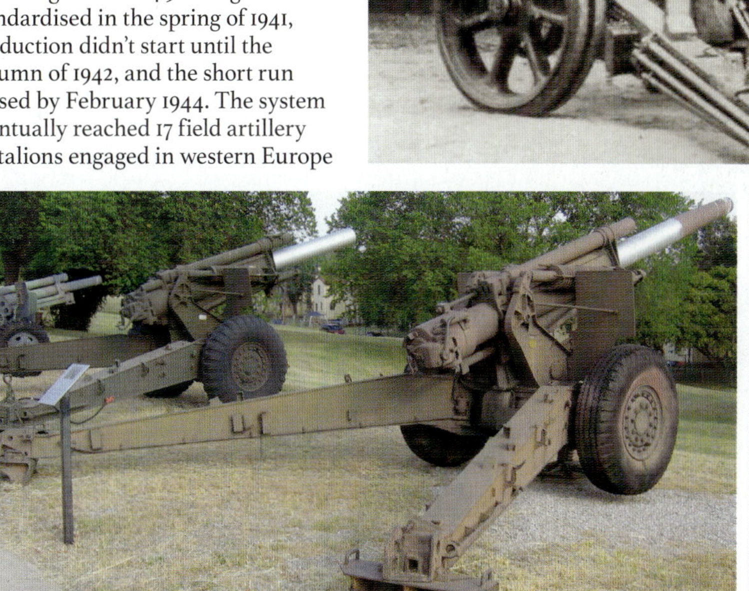

ABOVE: The 4.7-inch gun was a predecessor of the 4.5-inch that served during World War Two. (US GOVERNMENT VIA WIKIMEDIA COMMONS)

LEFT: An M1 4.5-inch gun is shown at right with a 155mm howitzer on display at Fort Sill, Oklahoma. (CREATIVE COMMONS STURMVOGEL66 VIA WIKIMEDIA COMMONS)

and was also deployed during the campaign in Italy in 1943. However, the gun was quickly deemed obsolete and largely replaced by the 155mm howitzer. By October 1945, it was being withdrawn from service. Although its performance was eclipsed by other more capable field guns, the M1 4.5-inch did provide critical fire support during early US campaigns in World War Two.

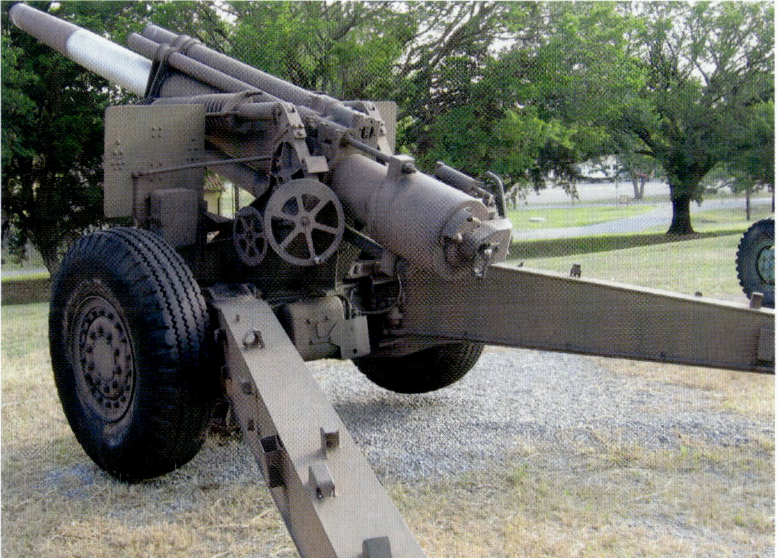

M1 4.5-inch Gun	
Country of Origin	USA
Calibre	4.5-inch (114mm)
Crew	10
Range	14.61 miles
Rate of Fire	4 rounds per minute
Number manufactured	426

LEFT: The M1 4.5mm gun was known for exceptional range but inferior ammunition. (CREATIVE COMMONS STURMVOGEL66 VIA WIKIMEDIA COMMONS)

Feld Kanone 16 nA

ABOVE: Soldiers of the Bundeswehr ride along as horses draw the Feld Kanone 16 nA during manoeuvres. (CREATIVE COMMONS BUNDESARCHIV BILD VIA WIKIMEDIA COMMONS)

RIGHT: Soldiers of the Bundeswehr operate a Feld Kanone 16 nA during exercises in the 1930s. (CREATIVE COMMONS BUNDESARCHIV BILD VIA WIKIMEDIA COMMONS)

During the inter-war years under the restrictions of the Versailles Treaty, the German Bundeswehr retained an abundance of its 77mm FK 16 field guns. These were redesigned with a new barrel to accommodate the next generation of high explosive ammunition. Thus, the 75mm Feld Kanone 16 nA became an early mainstay of the German land forces in the 1930s. The name literally translates to 75mm Field Gun 16 New Model.

Curiously, the effort to standardise German artillery retained some aspects of the earlier field guns of World War One and, in the case of the Feld Kanone 16 nA, this included the archaic wooden carriage. In this configuration, the gun was transportable only by horse teams, restricting its movement on the modern battlefield. Along with the spoked wooden wheels, the gun retained its box carriage and narrow traverse of only 4°, which further limited its use in real action. The appearance of the gun harkened back to earlier days as well, with two seats forward for artillerymen adjacent to the gun shield for use as the weapon was in tow.

Many of the re-barrelled 75mm guns were issued to cavalry units beginning in 1934, but these proved ponderous in the field and often unable to keep up with the horse soldiers, who were amazingly anachronistic in their own right. The gun was heavy at 3,360lb and this proved problematic in cross-country exercises, so many of the 75mm Feld Kanone 16 nA examples were transferred to training units or reserve formations.

Manufactured by Rheinmetall, the 75mm Feld Kanone 16 nA was generally considered a stopgap measure as it was one of the few artillery pieces the German military was allowed to retain under the terms of Versailles. After the fall of France and the Low Countries in 1940, a number of the World War One-vintage 77mm guns, handed over to the Belgian Army as war reparations, were captured and were re-barrelled by the Germans. Although it gave way to newer types such as the Feld Kanone 18, the 75mm Feld Kanone 16 nA was pressed into service as World War Two dragged on. Some were placed into the defences of the Atlantic Wall to contest the D-Day landings in 1944. Four examples were located in field entrenchments at the village of Breville and two were situated on Juno Beach to tackle Canadian forces.

RIGHT: The wooden spoked wheels of the Feld Kanone 16 nA are visible in this image at Fort Sill, Oklahoma. (CREATIVE COMMONS JASON LONG VIA WIKIMEDIA COMMONS)

Feld Kanone 16 nA	
Country of Origin	Germany
Calibre	75mm
Crew	8
Range	13,450 yards
Rate of Fire	9 rounds per minute
Number manufactured	fewer than 300

100mm K17

LEFT: This 100mm K17 field gun is on display at the US Army Field Artillery Museum, Fort Sill, Oklahoma. (CREATIVE COMMONS STURMVOGEL 66 VIA WIKIMEDIA COMMONS)

was eventually dropped. Along with a substantial range of more than 18,000 yards came a ponderous weight of over 7,200lb. Transport was accomplished by teams of six horses, and the barrel was separated from the carriage to accomplish overland movement. When level ground was located, the tube transporter was driven onto the carriage and lined up with the recoil system to be winched into position and locked in place.

The K17 was a follow-on to the earlier K14 with a lengthened barrel and simplified breech to a basic sliding wedge configuration. In the transition, elements of the earlier anti-aircraft role were retained, including equipment for a 360° traversing platform, 45° elevation and variable recoil. During World War One, the K17 proved an effective anti-personnel weapon with an expansive bursting radius of its high explosive and gas shells.

During World War Two, the K17 was one of several holdover types to see service. It shared common ammunition with standard weaponry of the German Navy and was considered suitable for coastal defence from the 1930s onward. It also saw service on the Eastern Front against the Red Army, although its lack of mobility restricted effectiveness in a war of rapid movement.

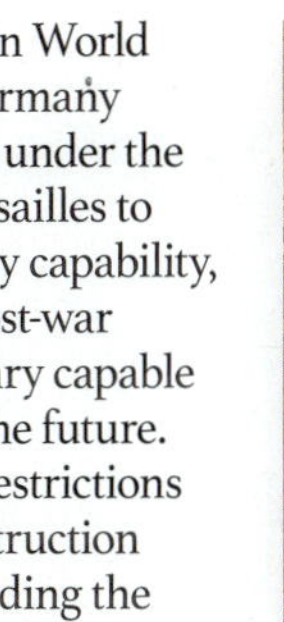

With its defeat in World War One, Germany was required under the Treaty of Versailles to drastically reduce its military capability, particularly the size of its post-war Bundeswehr and its weaponry capable of waging offensive war in the future.

Among those prominent restrictions imposed was the sale or destruction of much of its artillery, including the heavy 100mm K17 field gun. These were required either to be sold to other countries or rendered inoperable. While a number were transferred to Sweden and Romania, others were actually hidden and emerged once again in service during World War Two.

The 100MM K17 was originally in service from 1917-1918. Manufactured by the legendary Krupp works, the weapon was the last of a major line of field guns and intended for long range counter fire as well as a potential siege gun. An effort to convert the system for anti-aircraft purposes

LEFT: A British soldier inspects a captured German 100mm K17 gun in the field in 1918. (WESTERN NEWSPAPER UNION VIA WIKIMEDIA COMMONS)

BELOW: This 100mm K17 was placed in defensive position along the Atlantic Wall prior to World War Two. (CREATIVE COMMONS BUNDESARCHIV BILD VIA WIKIMEDIA COMMONS)

100mm K17	
Country of Origin	Germany
Calibre	105mm (actual)
Crew	6-8
Range	18,045 yards
Rate of Fire	4 rounds per minute
Number manufactured	192

100mm sK18

Interwar Product of Cooperation

Even amid the restrictions of the Treaty of Versailles that severely limited the German military in the years between the world wars, research and development of artillery continued in the country, first on a clandestine basis and then openly.

Between 1926 and 1930, famed German armaments manufacturers Rheinmetall and Krupp were each tasked with the development of a new long-range gun that would equip artillery batteries at the corps level of the Bundeswehr. When both submitted prototypes, the military vacillated as to which was superior and eventually settled on a hybrid that combined the best elements of both. As a result, the 100mm Kanone 18 became a standard weapon of medium artillery units by the late 1930s. While Rheinmetall supplied the barrel, the split trail carriage was a Krupp design.

The 100mm sK18 is distinguishable with its solid wheels marked by eight small holes, its short cradle for the barrel, equilibrators on either side of the barrel forward of the wheels and components of the recoil system that protrude above the barrel. It utilised a horizontal sliding block breech. The weapon entered service in 1934 but proved to be somewhat heavy for a single team of horses to transport cross-country. Therefore, the barrel and carriage were separated for transport until a half-track was determined capable of movement in tow with the piece intact.

In the field, the 100mm sK18 exhibited less than stellar performance. Its weight at more than 14,000lb during transport taxed scarce motorised options, while horse-drawn pieces required time

for assembly before commencing action. Further complications were uncovered with the gun itself, which was simply not powerful enough to fully execute the missions regularly at hand. Nevertheless, it was deployed in significant combat areas during World War Two, particularly in North Africa and the Nazi invasion of the Soviet Union.

The 100mm sK18 fired a relatively light shell which often lacked the necessary punch for sustained combat, particularly given the complicated size of the gun. An improved variant with a longer barrel was ready for production by 1941, but few were actually completed. As a result, the 100mm sK18 was relegated primarily to coastal defences.

100mm sK18	
Country of Origin	Germany
Calibre	105mm (actual)
Crew	6-10
Range	12 miles
Rate of Fire	6 rounds per minute
Number manufactured	1,433

150mm & 170mm K18

Long range from Rheinmetall and Krupp

Two objects of the German Army's focus on long range, heavy field artillery during World War Two were the 150mm and 170mm K18. As the Wehrmacht sought to replace its aged World War One-vintage guns in the 1930s, Rheinmetall began development of the 150mm Kanone 18 in 1933, with the first example entering service five years later.

The 150mm K18 was intended to replace the older K16 but offered only marginally improved performance, extending the range of the gun modestly, although the carriage was criticised due to the time required to transport and place the gun on a firing turntable before action could commence. In actual use, the weapon proved disappointing, because it didn't provide enough power for the exchange of assembly and transport headaches. Production ceased by 1943 and those examples available were distributed to coastal defence units.

By 1941, Krupp had entered the picture and offered the 170mm K18, also known as the K18 in MrsLaf

LEFT: German soldiers fire the 150mm K18 in the Soviet Union. (CREATIVE COMMONS BUNDESARCHIV BILD VIA WIKIMEDIA COMMONS)

(Cannon 18 on Motor Carriage). The 170mm K18 was designed along parallel lines with the 210mm Mörser, but soon supplanted it as a main production towed gun. Although the 210mm Mörser, which made its combat debut in 1939, was a potent and effective weapon, by 1941 the K18 was preferred because of its shell. At 150lb, the K18 high-explosive shell was lighter than the mortar at 249lb and deemed almost identical in destructive power. Therefore, production of the 210mm Mörser was discontinued by 1942 so that resources could be allocated to the K18.

Both the K18 and the 210mm Mörser shared a common double recoil system, the primary recoil being attached to the barrel to absorb some of the shock, while the secondary was incorporated into the carriage. The result was improved accuracy as the carriage was displaced only slightly during repeated firing. The K18 also offered the advantage of being transportable as a single piece over short distances, although longer transport required two-piece disassembly. In the latter case, a system of ramps and winches facilitated firing preparation.

During World War Two, the 170mm K18 was widely utilised by the German Army and developed a reputation as a reliable and effective weapon. Instances are documented in which Allied troops actually used captured examples during the fighting in North Africa and in western Europe when their own ammunition supplies for artillery were slowed by lengthy distances in the 1944 advance toward the German frontier.

LEFT: German soldiers fire a 170mm K18 during an attack against the Anzio beachhead in Italy, 1944. (NATIONAL DIGITAL ARCHIVES OF POLAND VIA WIKIMEDIA COMMONS)

LEFT: Artillerymen brace for the report of a 170mm K18 during the North Africa campaign. (CREATIVE COMMONS BUNDESARCHIV BILD VIA WIKIMEDIA COMMONS)

K18 150mm & 170mm	
Country of Origin	Germany
Calibre	149.1mm & 172.5mm (actual)
Crew	8 & 10
Range	15.22 & 18.4 miles
Rate of Fire	2 rounds per minute
Number manufactured	101 & 338

M1931/37 122mm

Product of Petrov Design Bureau

ABOVE: Russian troops on the offensive follow an M1931/37 122mm gun being towed by a tracked vehicle through snow. (CREATIVE COMMONS RIA NOVOSTY VIA WIKIMEDIA COMMONS)

RIGHT: Red Army soldiers fire their M1931/37 122mm gun in defence of Moscow in 1941. (CREATIVE COMMONS RIA NOVOSTY VIA WIKIMEDIA COMMONS)

BELOW: This captured M1931/37 122mm gun is shown in towing configuration in a German photo. (CREATIVE COMMONS BUNDESARCHIV BILD VIA WIKIMEDIA COMMONS)

The Soviet Union manufactured vast quantities of artillery during World War Two, often improving on existing designs. One such example was the M1931/37 122mm gun, which married the barrel of the M1931 field gun with the carriage of the M1937 ML-20 152mm gun howitzer. Also known as the A-19, this weapon was conceived to address some shortcomings of the M1931, including an elevation mechanism that was prone to malfunction and tyres that were solid rather than pneumatic.

The Petrov Design Bureau handled the conversion and the first of the new guns underwent trials in the autumn of 1938. Adopted for regular service in April 1939, the gun and carriage combination proved satisfactory in combat conditions. Its long range was suited for bombarding enemy troop and armour concentrations, as well as in the counter battery fire role. Towing was accomplished in a single piece either using a wheeled or tracked vehicle, and a limber was employed to provide support for the ends of the split trail carriage and its leaf spring suspension. During transport, the barrel was retracted to provide load balance and shorten the length of the long tandem.

The 122mm gun utilised an interrupted screw breech and fired a variety of shells with separate loading of propellant with cased charge ammunition. The carriage also included an equilibrator and gun shield that provided some protection for the crew against small arms fire and shell fragments.

In action, the M1931/37 122mm gun was effective against its intended targets and was sometimes pressed into the anti-tank role during early fighting on the Eastern Front during World War Two. Originally deployed at the corps level, the gun was present in large numbers along the front while also being distributed to reserves. A tank gun variant, the D-25, was produced by 1943 and proven capable of defeating the heavy German PzKpfw. VI Tiger tank at optimal range. In the waning months of the Great Patriotic War, an M1931/37 was given the honour of firing the first shot of the direct Red Army assault on Berlin on April 20, 1945. German forces captured quantities of the weapon during the opening phases of Operation Barbarossa and pressed some into service as the 122mm K.390(r). Some examples were sold to Fascist Spain.

Production of the weapon took place from 1939 to 1946, and many survived the war and were present during conflicts of the Cold War in the latter half of the 20th Century.

M1931/37 122mm	
Country of Origin	Soviet Union
Calibre	122mm
Crew	9
Range	12.7 miles
Rate of Fire	6 rounds per minute
Number manufactured	2,926

M1944 100mm

The M1944 100mm field gun, also known as the BS-3, was a versatile weapon of the Red Army during World War Two that was determined to play a key role not only with the light artillery brigades of Soviet tank armies in fire support but also as an effective anti-tank gun.

Throughout the Great Patriotic War, Soviet field artillery increased in potency and mobility. The BS-3 was fielded in 1944 following a programme of improvement led by the engineering and design team under VG Grabin, head of Josef Stalin Factory No 92 at Gorky. Grabin was also known for the development of the famed ZiS-3 76.2mm gun.

Based on the B-34 naval gun, the BS-3 entered production in early 1944 and was deployed along with the ZiS-3 to the corps level of tank armies. The gun fired a smaller shell than the contemporary M 1931/37 122mm and was, therefore, less powerful. However, it was more mobile and possessed a higher rate of fire. It employed a semi-automatic vertical sliding wedge breech and hydropneumatic recoil while atop a split trail carriage. Its barrel length stretched 17ft, 6in, and the weapon weighed over 8,000lb. Despite its relative heft, the gun

M1944 100mm	
Country of Origin	Soviet Union
Calibre	100mm
Crew	6-8
Range	12.42 miles
Rate of Fire	10 rounds per minute
Number manufactured	1,481

ABOVE: The imposing barrel of the M1944 100mm gun is prominent in this example on display in Moscow. (CREATIVE COMMONS DMITRY IVANOV VIA WIKIMEDIA COMMONS)

LEFT: This BS-3 100mm gun is on display at the Batey ha-Osef Museum in Tel Aviv, Israel. (CREATIVE COMMONS BUKVOED VIA WIKIMEDIA COMMONS)

could be towed by vehicles and was considered highly mobile. It utilised high explosive shells along with armour piercing and fragmentation rounds.

In the anti-tank role, the BS-3 was capable of destroying the PzKpfw. VI Tiger tank from distances up to 5,200ft. By the end of World War Two, the Red Army had equipped 13 anti-tank brigades and three corps artillery brigades with the powerful gun, and its post-war career has stretched into the 21st Century as examples have been observed during the ongoing war between Russia and Ukraine. Its career as a frontline weapon of the Red Army had begun to wane by the 1950s as it was replaced by the T-12 and 85mm D-48 in the anti-tank role.

As recently as 2012, it was known that at least 12 BS-3s were on station in the Kurile Islands in defensive positions. Production ended in 1951.

The long split trail carriage is a notable feature of the BS-3 field artillery and anti-tank gun. (CREATIVE COMMONS BUKVOED VIA WIKIMEDIA COMMONS)

M1939 Divisional Gun 76mm USV

Critical Redesign for the Red Army

M1939 Divisional Gun 76mm USV	
Country of Origin	Soviet Union
Calibre	76.2mm
Crew	5
Range	8.26 miles
Rate of Fire	15 rounds per minute
Number manufactured	9,812

ABOVE LEFT: Soviet soldiers rush forward to position their M1939 76mm field gun for firing. (RUSSIAN FEDERATION EMMANUIL EVZERIKHIN VIA WIKIMEDIA COMMONS)

ABOVE RIGHT: An M1939 76mm USV is towed through the mud on the Eastern Front in the spring of 1942. (RUSSIAN FEDERATION MIKHAIL SAMOYLOVICH BERNSHTEIN VIA WIKIMEDIA COMMONS)

With the outbreak of World War Two, the Soviet Red Army's best light artillery was the 76.2mm Divisional Gun M1939 USV, an improvement over the earlier M1936 F-22, which had been designed originally as a universal gun to perform in the anti-aircraft, field artillery and anti-tank roles.

By 1937, the Soviet military establishment had become disenchanted with the older M1902/30 and its replacement, the M1936 F-22, and undertook the quest for a better weapon. The No. 92 Plant design bureau, under the direction of VG Grabin, won the race to develop the new weapon over two competing bureaus. Its designation as F-22 USV indicated that it was an improvement over the existing M1936, but in reality it was a completely new design, with a shortened L/41 barrel carried atop the M1933 split trail carriage, a completely re-engineered recoil system with recuperator cylinders above and below the barrel and other modifications. However, in service, shortcomings were revealed, including significant weight at 3,240lb and poorly located controls for elevation and sighting.

The M1939 76mm USV entered production that year and more than 1,200 were completed by the end of 1940. Production ceased in 1941 as Red Army focus shifted to higher calibre guns at the divisional level. However, the German invasion of the Soviet Union in June 1941 spurred an abrupt return of the type to the assembly line. More examples were built into 1942, but the M1939 was gradually replaced by the end of that year with the ZiS-3.

One major cause for this replacement was the large number of M1939s captured by the Germans on the Eastern Front during the opening months of World War Two. Those in German possession were often placed in service as the 76.2mm FK 297(r) or FK39(r). German forces also captured the production facilities that supplied the M1933 carriage, substantially impeding the ability of the Soviets to complete new M1939 weapons.

The M1939 76mm USV carriage incorporated the metal wheels and rubber tyres of the ZiS-5 3-tonne cargo truck, while the gun itself featured a vertical sliding breech block and cradle originated by the Swedish company Bofors. The barrel was fabricated to accept standard Model 1900 ammunition, which enabled the M1939 to utilise stockpiles of older shells.

In addition to the German Army, Finnish and Romanian forces also deployed captured M1939s.

RIGHT: Manufactured in Stalingrad in 1941, this example of the M1939 76mm gun on display at the Hämeenlinna Artillery Museum in Finland. (CREATIVE COMMONS BALCER-COMMONSWIKI VIA WIKIMEDIA COMMONS)

M1942 Divisional Gun 76mm ZiS-3

Long Service Life for Soviet Mainstay

Although its development was undertaken without the sanction of the Soviet military establishment or state approval, the M1942 Divisional Gun 76mm ZiS-3 became the most widely deployed Red Army medium field artillery piece of World War Two. Its origins lay in the necessity of replacing the heavier and more costly M1939 F-22 USV.

The initiator of the new design was VG Grabin and the designation of ZiS (Zavod imeni Stalina) or "factory named after Stalin" was an honorary title bestowed on the Plant No 92 design bureau at Gorky, where the first of the type were built. Steady production of the ZiS-3 began in December 1941 as the Red Army had reeled before the Nazi invasion of the previous summer. However, the gun remained sidelined for a while as the Red Army refused to accept it for frontline use without proper testing.

Grabin used his persuasive capabilities to convince the military that the ZiS-3 should be tested in the field, and a quick demonstration before Premier Josef Stalin led to an impromptu five days of trials in February 1942. From there, the weapon became a mainstay of the Red Army.

The ZiS-3 design was rather basic, combining the proven 76.2mm gun with the split trail carriage of the light 57mm ZiS-2 anti-tank gun. A large slotted muzzle brake facilitated the combination by reducing recoil and stress on the carriage frame while also providing better accuracy, range and penetrating capability of armour piercing ammunition. The weapon was capable of taking on most German armoured vehicles and tanks in the field. Its high rate of fire and good muzzle velocity made it a worthy support weapon for infantry with primary firing missions against enemy troop concentrations, artillery emplacements, bunkers and vehicles.

The ZiS-3 was mobile, compact, cheap to build and versatile. It was easy to maintain in combat conditions and crews required minimal training to operate the weapon efficiently.

Stalin called the ZiS-3 "a masterpiece of artillery systems design." It was easily towed into combat zones by heavy duty jeeps or four-wheel drive trucks such as the Lend Lease Dodge ¾-tonne that also served as transportation for the crew and accompanying ammunition. For relocation over short distances, the weapon was sometimes even moved by sheer manpower.

Production of the ZiS-3 ceased with the end of World War Two and the gun was substantially replaced in the Red Army by the 85mm D44 field gun. Many were exported to Soviet satellite countries during the Cold War, and it is known to have served in both the Korean and Vietnam conflicts.

ABOVE: These 76mm ZiS-3 guns take part in a victory parade in the spring of 1945. (RUSSIAN FEDERATION GEORGY UGRINOVICH VIA WIKIMEDIA COMMONS)

LEFT: A ZiS-3 76mm gun crew fires through a hole in a brick wall in Poznan, Poland. (RUSSIAN FEDERATION VIA WIKIMEDIA COMMONS)

M1942 Divisional Gun 76mm ZiS-3	
Country of Origin	Soviet Union
Calibre	76.2mm
Crew	5-7
Range	8.25 miles
Rate of Fire	25 rounds per minute
Number manufactured	103,000 or more

BELOW: German soldiers accompanied by a Tiger tank pass an abandoned ZiS-3 field gun on the Eastern Front. (CREATIVE COMMONS BUNDESARCHIV BILD VIA WIKIMEDIA COMMONS)

Type 90 75mm

Japan's Most Modern Artillery

ABOVE: British soldiers inspect a Type 90 75mm gun captured during fighting in Burma. (COLLECTIONS OF THE IMPERIAL WAR MUSEUMS VIA WIKIMEDIA COMMONS)

RIGHT: This Type 90 75mm field gun resides in the Military Museum of the Chinese People's Revolution in Beijing. (CREATIVE COMMONS MORIO VIA WIKIMEDIA COMMONS)

According to some observers, the Type 90 75mm field gun was the most modern weapon of its type fielded by the Imperial Japanese Army during World War Two. The Type 90 derived its name from the its acceptance for service in the army in 1930.

Designed largely along the lines of the French Schneider 85mm gun Model 1927, the Type 90 saw action in both the Second Sino-Japanese War which began in 1937 and the series of Japanese armed clashes with the Soviet Red Army along the border with Manchuria in 1939. Although the Japanese military had depended on German-manufactured Krupp artillery prior to World War Two and the Type 90 was intended to replace the earlier Type 38 75mm gun, its relative expense and logistical constraints prevented the completion of this exercise. Thus, the Type 38 also served through World War Two.

The Type 90 was the only Japanese field gun to incorporate a muzzle brake, and it demonstrated high muzzle velocity with 50° muzzle traverse. These characteristics made it effective in the anti-tank role, while it also served as a direct infantry support weapon against enemy troop concentrations, hardened targets such as bunkers or fortified buildings and communication centres. During the US advance across the Pacific from 1943 to 1945, the Type 90 and Type 38 served simultaneously in opposition to the US landings in the Philippines, Iwo Jima and Okinawa.

The Type 90 operated either with a wooden carriage for horse-drawn transport or with a reinforced suspension carriage and rubber tyres for movement by towing vehicle. The weapon required a high degree of precision in its components and was complicated to produce, which contributed to the failure to manufacture the weapon in expected numbers. It weighed 3,086lb in firing disposition, its barrel measured 9ft, 6in, and its primary high explosive shell weighed 14½lb. The split trail carriage was anchored in firing position with the use of metal stakes rather than spades, requiring a significant investment of time to move from one location to another. The gun was operated with a horizontal sliding block breech.

Type 90 75mm	
Country of Origin	Japan
Calibre	75mm
Crew	7
Range	9.3 miles
Rate of Fire	10-12 rounds per minute
Number manufactured	786

RIGHT: The Japanese Type 90 75mm field gun was patterned after a French Schneider model. (CREATIVE COMMONS STURMVOGEL 66 VIA WIKIMEDIA COMMONS)

Type 92 100mm

Japanese Link to French Design

Like its contemporary companion the Type 90 75mm field gun, the Type 92 100mm (actually 105mm) gun was of French lineage. The French Schneider company contributed to the development of the weapon during the 1920s, and it served during the Second Sino-Japanese War, the Soviet Border War in Manchuria in 1939, and in World War Two.

So named because it entered service in the year 2592 according to the Japanese calendar, the development of the Type 92 was undertaken in 1923 as a long range improvement over the 75mm field guns then in widespread use with the Imperial Japanese Army. Intended to replace the Type 14 100mm gun, it was initially plagued by setbacks involving weight and other requirements as the army command sought to increase mobility and range with the new gun.

With the assistance of Schneider, a prototype was finally completed in 1932, and following a testing regimen the Type 92 was placed in production. By 1934, the gun had been accepted as standard issue.

Type 92 100mm	
Country of Origin	Japan
Calibre	105mm (actual)
Crew	5-7
Range	20,000 yards
Rate of Fire	8 rounds per minute
No. Manufactured	200 approximately

The weapon became known for its tremendous range, hurling a 35-pound long range high explosive shell an impressive 20,000 yards or 11.36 miles. Its long slender barrel measured 15 feet, four inches, which complicated transport in the field, while it operated with a somewhat unique three-step interrupted thread breech block and hydropneumatic recoil system.

The Type 92 was typically transported by prime mover or five-ton cargo truck, its split trail carriage fit for towing with rather sizable wooden wheels and rubber tyres that were of solid construction. One of the weapon's pronounced shortcomings was the use of spade plates attached to each trail leg. These required the arduous work of being hammered into the ground so that the recoil could be sufficiently absorbed, and the time element seriously limited the mobility of the gun.

Sufficiently up to the task of long range suppressive and counter battery fire, the Type 92 entered combat for the first time against the Soviets at the lengthy Battle of Nomonhan in Manchuria. It was later used to pound U.S. positions on the Bataan peninsula and the island of Corregidor during the 1942 conquest of the Philippine Islands and was shipped to the embattled island of Guadalcanal in the Solomons to shell the vital Henderson Field.

The Type 92 was manufactured at the Osaka Arsenal from the prototype to the end of World War Two in 1945, although it was completed in relatively low numbers.

TOP: The anchor spades are visible on the split trail carriage in this image of the Type 92 100mm gun. (U.S. WAR DEPARTMENT VIA WIKIMEDIA COMMONS)

ABOVE: This Japanese Type 92 100mm field gun is displayed on the grounds of the Istana, official residence of the president of Singapore. (CREATIVE COMMONS SENGKANG VIA WIKIMEDIA COMMONS)

LEFT: The breech of the Type 92 100mm gun was engineered with a unique design. (U.S. WAR DEPARTMENT VIA WIKIMEDIA COMMONS)

Canon de 75 Modele 1897

Famed as the French 75

Known more familiarly as the French 75 or the Soixante-Quinze, the Canon de 75 Modele 1897 is an iconic field gun and acknowledged by many historians as the first modern weapon of its type.

Introduced at the turn of the 20th Century, the field gun is known for its rapid rate of fire and its distinguishing features that separated it from earlier types, rendering many of them immediately obsolete. Its 75mm bore was the work of Colonel Albert Deport of the French Army, and its basic configuration was completed in 1894. The gun entered service with the French Army in March 1898.

Its hydropneumatic recoil system was revolutionary in that the barrel and breech recoiled via rollers while the carriage remained steady. The result was a stable firing platform that increased rate of fire and accuracy while eliminating the need for the crew to wrestle the gun back into position after the discharge of a single round. Two cylinders operated the recoil system, one which contained oil and damped the gun's recoil while a second cylinder utilised air pressure to return the breech and barrel to firing position.

The French 75 was also known for its fast-action rotating screw breech invented by Swedish industrialist Thorsten Nordenfelt and built under license in France. Further enhancing battlefield performance, the weapon utilised a single ammunition round with shell and powder charge incorporated rather than separately loaded shell and propellant. Therefore, its rate of fire was better than other contemporary field artillery pieces.

The French 75 was a mainstay of Allied land forces during World War One, and was highly mobile before

the period of trench warfare on the Western Front. Its use among the Allies was widespread and, by the end of World War One, the US Army had received about 2,000 of them. Effective against soft targets such as troop concentrations and supply centres, the gun also delivered noxious gas shells. It was also mounted on flatbed trucks as an anti-aircraft weapon.

A half-century later, the French 75 remained relevant during World War Two. Despite new developments in field artillery, the French Army still fielded roughly 4,500 of the guns in 1939. After the seizure of Poland and the fall of France, German forces redeployed captured examples as the 75mm Pak 97/38. In the US Army, the horse-drawn guns were modified for towing by trucks, including those guns procured from the French and built under license in the US. Modernised with the split trail carriage M2A2 and pneumatic tyres to facilitate rapid movement, the French 75 was

also sometimes installed aboard the M3 half-track as a tank destroyer, designated the M3 Gun Motor Carriage. In 1940, the British Army supplemented artillery losses in France with the purchase of 895 examples of the French 75 and millions of rounds of ammunition from the US.

While the French 75 was rapidly becoming functionally obsolete during World War Two, it remained active throughout the conflict and is considered today an outstanding weapon of superior performance.

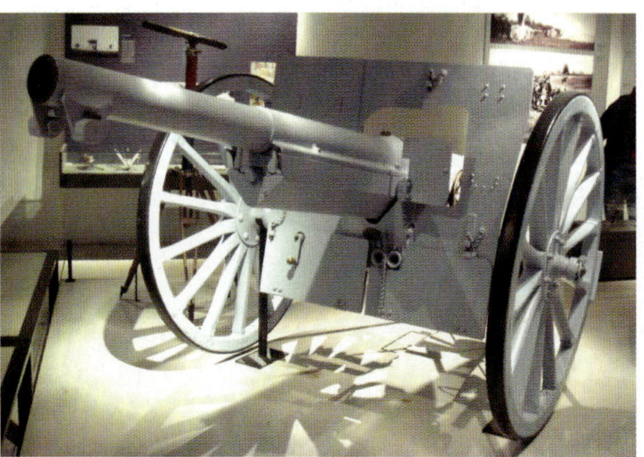

Canon de 75 Modele 1897	
Country of Origin	France
Calibre	75mm
Crew	6
Range	12,000 yards
Rate of Fire	4 rounds per minute sustained
Number manufactured	21,000 or more

Canon de 105L Mle 1936 Schneider

Vanguard of French Field Guns

Along with the 20mm Mle 1939 anti-aircraft gun, the Canon de 105L Mle 1936 built by the defence contractor Schneider et Cie was the most modern field artillery piece in the French arsenal at the beginning of World War Two. However, only a relative few were manufactured and many of those were purchased by the Romanian Army prior to the outbreak of hostilities.

The Mle 1936 entered service with the French military in the mid-1930s and it was manufactured in two configurations. One of these utilised wooden spoked wheels for the box trail carriage to facilitate transport by horse. The other was built with steel wheels and rubber tyres for vehicle towing. The weapon was known for its relatively quick firing capability with its interrupted screw breech, although ammunition was separately loaded with shell and propellant. Its standard shell weighed 35lb and its range of nearly 17,500 yards was still inferior to that of contemporary German long range artillery.

The Mle 1936 was utilised throughout World War Two with the Romanian Army, an Axis belligerent, which received 144 of an order for 180 prior to the outbreak of the conflict. With the fall of France in 1940, a number of the weapons were captured by the Germans, redesignated the 105mm schwere Kanone 332(f), and deployed primarily in coastal defences, including the Atlantic Wall in Normandy.

The French Army counted 159 examples of the Mle 1936 in its inventory on the eve of World War Two, and these were assigned to organic corps artillery formations. The barrel extended 12ft, 10in, and the heavier horse-drawn version weighed more than 7,800lb.

Canon de 105L Mle 1936 Schneider	
Country of Origin	France
Calibre	105mm
Crew	7
Range	17,498 yards
Rate of Fire	4 rounds per minute
Number manufactured	approximately 300

ABOVE: The Mle 1936 on display at the Fort de Fermont museum in France. (CREATIVE COMMONS ALFVANBEEM VIA WIKIMEDIA COMMONS)

LEFT: A French crew fires its Mle 1936 in action during December 1939. (EUROPEAN UNION VIA WIKIMEDIA COMMONS)

BELOW: A battery of French Mle 105mm field guns belches smoke and flame early in World War Two. (EUROPEAN UNION VIA WIKIMEDIA COMMONS)

After World War Two, the French used the Mle 1936 during military operations in Algeria and Indochina. Those examples that were left with the Romanians were upgraded with modern carriage attributes and were in service through the 1990s as training pieces. These were operated until the supplies of available ammunition were exhausted.

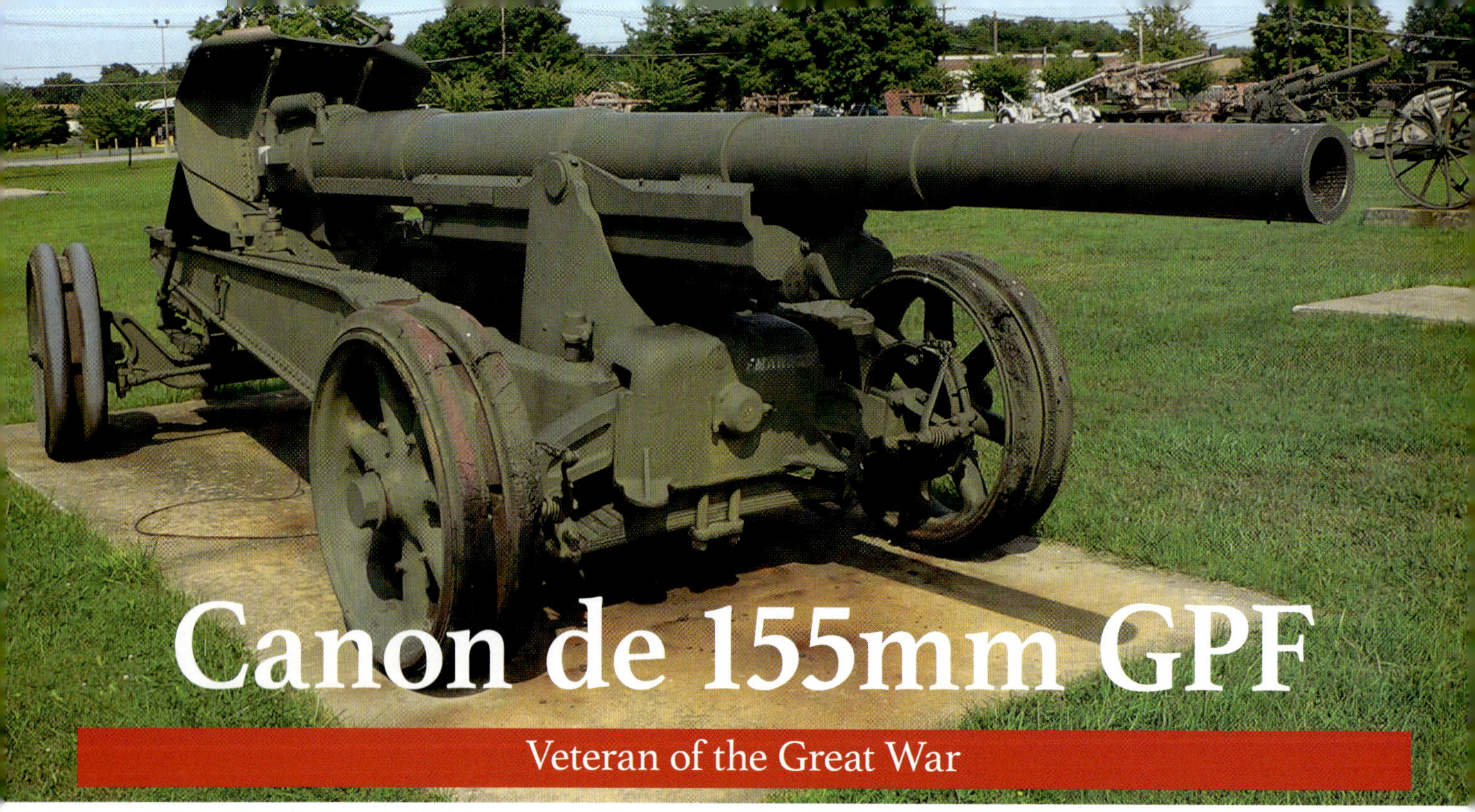

Canon de 155mm GPF

Veteran of the Great War

ABOVE: This example of the Canon de 155mm GPF is displayed at Aberdeen Proving Ground, Maryland. (CREATIVE COMMONS MARK PELLEGRINI VIA WIKIMEDIA COMMONS)

Like many other field artillery weapons in World War Two, the Canon de 155mm GPF was a holdover from World War One. The gun's name honours its developer, Colonel Louis Filloux, and GPF stands for Grande Puissance Filloux, denoting its high calibre.

As the requirement for modern heavy field artillery grew amid the French Army combat experience in World War One, Filloux responded to an urgent situation. The 155mm GPF was rushed into production and pressed hurriedly into service, becoming the standard heavy field artillery of the French Army from 1917. In combat conditions, it was praised as one of the best artillery pieces fielded by the Allies. The 155mm GPF was easily recognised by its long barrel that stretched 20ft, its split trail carriage invented by French Colonel Joseph-Albert Deport (who was also involved in the development of the iconic French 75) and its maximum range of 21,325 yards hurling a 95lb shell that was separately loaded with propellant through the gun's interrupted screw breech. The unique carriage differed from earlier models with its majority of cast components rather than riveted, machined or pressed parts.

During World War One, US forces acquired the 155mm GPF and manufactured a close derivative, the M1918, into World War Two. The US Marine Corps also employed the weapon as standard until 1942, when supplies of the new 155mm M1 Long Tom supplanted it.

When war broke out in 1939, the French Army possessed approximately 450 examples of the 155mm GPF and these were active through the fall of France in the spring of 1940. Captured field pieces were redesignated the 155mm Kanone 418(f) by the Germans and repurposed largely as coastal defence guns. On D-Day, at least 50 examples of the gun were trained against Allied forces landing on the beaches of Normandy. Famously, a battery of six 155mm GPF guns was the target of the American Ranger assault at Pointe du Hoc.

In the Pacific theatre, US forces utilised the 155mm GPF in fortifications at the entrance to Manila Bay in the Philippines and on the Bataan peninsula and the island of Corregidor. From 1944 through the end of the war, the gun was sometimes mounted on the chassis of the M3 medium tank and designated the self-propelled M12 gun motor carriage.

Canon de 155mm GPF	
Country of Origin	France
Calibre	155mm
Crew	10
Range	21,325 yards
Rate of Fire	3 rounds per minute
Number manufactured	approximately 450

BELOW RIGHT: A 155mm GPF with a Panama mount for coastal defence at Garden Island, Western Australia, 1943. (GOVERNMENT OF AUSTRALIA VIA WIKIMEDIA COMMONS)

BELOW: British soldiers try to move a French-built 155mm GPF through mud after capturing it from the Germans in Italy, 1944. (COLLECTIONS OF THE IMPERIAL WAR MUSEUMS VIA WIKIMEDIA COMMONS)

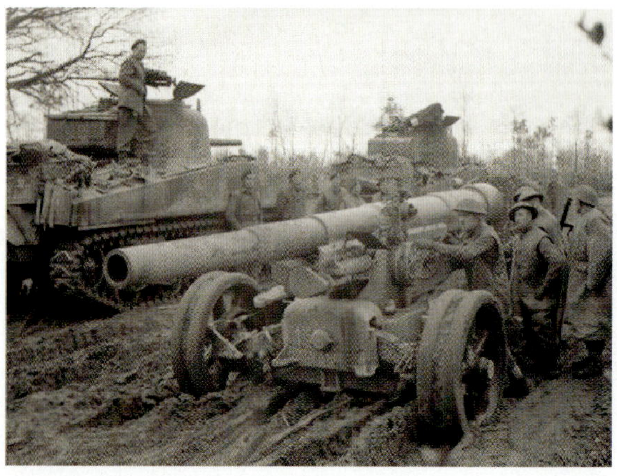

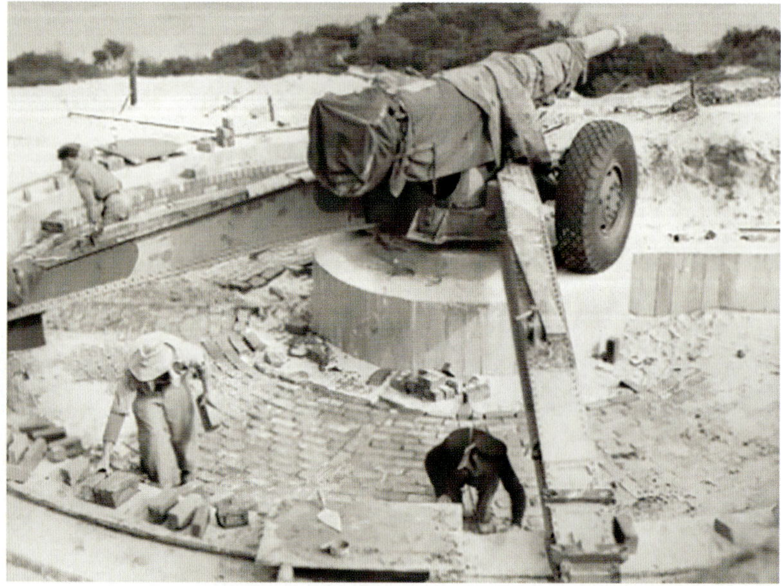

Ordnance QF 18-pounder

With its roots in the Second Boer War, the Ordnance QF 18-pounder was introduced to service in 1904 and became a workhorse of the Royal Artillery during World War One.

The gun was developed as the result of an equipment committee formed to identify the characteristics of a modern British field gun to raise the army's artillery to parity with that of other European nations. Arms manufacturers were invited to compete for the contract, but those that submitted specimens were informed that each was lacking in some respect. Therefore, a collaboration arose with a new weapon designated QF for 'quick firing' and incorporating the Armstrong barrel, Royal Ordnance ammunition capacity, sighting and elevation equipment and the Vickers recoil system.

The QF 18-pounder weighed 2,825lb, operated with a single motion screw breech with cartridge extractor and fired a round weighing 23lb with shell and propellant fixed together to a maximum range of 6,500 yards in the gun's Mark I and II variants. The barrel was 7ft, 8in

Ordnance QF 18-Pounder	
Country of Origin	Great Britain
Calibre	18-pounder (84mm)
Crew	6
Range	6,525 yards (Mk I & II)
Rate of Fire	4 rounds per minute sustained
Number manufactured	10,469

long with a bore of 84mm, while the hydropneumatic recoil system improved stabilisation and accuracy. The carriage was initially a pole trail type, but this was modified to box trails in later variants to improve elevation and range.

During World War Two, Territorial Army units were primary users in the British ranks, although some frontline units did operate the gun during the East Africa campaign, the fighting in North Africa and in western Europe, where more than 200 were lost to the Germans in 1940 with the evacuation of the British Expeditionary Force from Dunkirk and in other actions. The QF 18-pounder was present during early battles in the China-Burma-India theatre, firing some of the initial rounds of the Pacific War while fielded by Indian troops. Most of the guns in Asia were lost with the Japanese capture of Singapore and Hong Kong. These losses were later made good with the introduction of the QF 25-pounder.

The retirement of the 18-pounder from combat was largely accomplished by 1942. Remaining examples were used as coastal defence guns and for training purposes.

ABOVE: French officers inspect an 18-pounder gun in the town of Orchies, France, in April **1940.** (COLLECTIONS OF THE IMPERIAL WAR MUSEUMS VIA WIKIMEDIA COMMONS)

FAR LEFT: This QF 18-pounder is shown in later split trail carriage configuration during 1938 manoeuvres. (BRITISH ARMY COLLECTIONS OF THE IMPERIAL WAR MUSEUMS VIA WIKIMEDIA COMMONS)

LEFT: This 18-pounder field gun with modified shield is being towed by a Morris tractor. (BRITISH ARMY COLLECTIONS OF THE IMPERIAL WAR MUSEUMS VIA WIKIMEDIA COMMONS)

Ordnance QF 25-pounder

Lasting Fame in the Field

The British Army's Ordnance QF 25-pounder was one of the great field artillery pieces to emerge during World War Two. Its inception was the product of a concerted effort to replace the venerable QF 18-pounder and the 4.5-inch howitzer, both mainstays of the army during World War One, so the new 25-pounder incorporated characteristics of both a field gun and howitzer, capable of firing at higher trajectories up 45° regularly and 80° with adapter equipment and dug in positioning or on a flat trajectory even in an anti-tank role if needed.

The 25-pounder was primarily a field artillery support weapon, hitting enemy troop concentrations and supply centres or providing direct fire against strongpoints along the front line. Its development was undertaken in the 1930s, although funding restrictions slowed progress. The firing platform of the 18-pounder and other elements of the older gun were incorporated.

The firing platform, hydropneumatic recoil and spade located in several split trail or box trail carriage variants made for a quite stable and accurate firing sequence. The barrel was 15ft, 1in long with a bore of 87.63mm, and the shell was fired separately from the propellant charge. Although this process seemed to slow the rate of fire, it provided the advantage of more accurate targeting. The high explosive shell weighed 25lb and ammunition was carried in a separate trailer. Both gun and trailer were typically towed by a 4X4 Field Artillery Tractor, nicknamed 'Quad', such as the Morris C8.

The 25-pounder entered service with the British Army in 1940 during the early days of World War Two and saw action in virtually every theatre where British and Commonwealth troops were engaged. Both infantry and armoured formations fielded the weapon, and numerous variants of gun and carriage were manufactured before production ceased in 1945, although the career of the 25-pounder stretched on for decades.

It played a prominent role during the North Africa campaign and was notably employed in the epic Battle of El Alamein in October 1942. Commonwealth troops were heavily dependent on the 25-pounder during the fighting in Italy, while the gun was also employed by Greek artillery regiments fighting Axis forces at the Battle of Rimini in 1944. It was a mainstay during the Allied drive from the Normandy beaches into the Third Reich in the final months of World War Two in Europe, and was sent to the jungles of New Guinea in a smaller light variant dubbed the 25-pounder Short.

The versatility, mobility and durability of the 25-pounder earned praise from friend and foe alike, and it is considered one of the finest artillery pieces of World War Two.

Ordnance QF 25-Pounder	
Country of Origin	Great Britain
Calibre	25-pounder (87.63mm)
Crew	6
Range	13,400 yards
Rate of Fire	8 rounds per minute
Number manufactured	13,000 minimum

BL 4.5-inch & 5.5-inch Medium Guns

Commonwealth Regimental Firepower

The British and Commonwealth armies deployed two medium field artillery pieces during World War Two, and the primary function of the BL 4.5-inch and 5.5-inch guns was counter battery fire. While the destructive power of their respective shells was not as robust as other weapons, the large fragments they produced suited them well in their main fire missions.

The 4.5-inch medium gun was in service by the late 1930s as a replacement for the earlier BL 60-pounder that had seen its best days, most of the available examples worn from extreme use. The 5.5-inch gun was the result of a directive issued in January 1939 to replace existing 6-inch howitzers with a range of 16,000 yards.

Both weapons were issued at the regimental level with the 4.5-inch closely resembling its 60-pounder predecessor. The 4.5-inch gun weighed nearly 13,000lb in firing configuration, and its distinctive barrel stretched 15ft, 9in, substantially longer than that of the 5.5-inch gun whose barrel was 13ft, 9in. The 5.5-inch gun weighed nearly 14,000lb. Both weapons utilised the Welin breech and the Asbury interrupted screw breechlock

mechanism similar to that of some naval guns. Some difficulties were encountered in the field, resulting in them replaced with earlier World War One equipment. The guns shared the same carriage, variants of which were noted along the lines of cast rather than riveted components. Both the 4.5- and 5.5-inch were towed primarily by the AEC Matador 4X4 artillery tractor.

The 4.5-inch gun entered service in 1938 and was fielded by both British and Canadian medium artillery regiments. Roughly half such Canadian regiments used the 4.5-inch. The weapons were present in rather small quantity, with at least one regiment attached to the British Expeditionary Force in 1940. They were further used in the Battle of

BL 4.5-Inch & 5.5-Inch Medium Guns	
Country of Origin	Great Britain
Calibre	4.5-inch (114mm) & 5.5-inch (140mm)
Crew	10 each
Range	20,500 yards & 16,200 yards
Rate of Fire	3 & 2 rounds per minute
Number manufactured	650 & 5,000

France, North Africa and in Greece. The Mk II variant, which differed only slightly from the original Mk I, also served in North Africa, Italy and western Europe.

The 5.5-inch gun entered service in 1941and reached North Africa the following year. British and Free French regiments served 20 of them during the Battle of El Alamein in October 1942. Numerous Commonwealth artillery regiments fielded the 5.5-incher, which was also deployed across the globe. After World War Two, it replaced the 4.5-inch as standard.

TOP: A Canadian crewman stands beside a stockpile of 5.5-inch medium gun shells. (NATIONAL LIBRARY AND ARCHIVES OF CANADA VIA WIKIMEDIA COMMONS)

ABOVE: A British BL 4.5-inch medium gun fires in the desert to the south of El Alamein. (COLLECTIONS OF THE IMPERIAL WAR MUSEUMS VIA WIKIMEDIA COMMONS)

LEFT: A crew fires a 5.5-inch medium gun near the front lines in Italy, 1944. (COLLECTIONS OF THE IMPERIAL WAR MUSEUMS VIA WIKIMEDIA COMMONS)

Ansaldo 149/40 M1935

Overpromised and Undelivered

ABOVE: The Ansaldo 149/40 M1935 was produced in low numbers as a heavy field gun. (GOVERNMENT OF ITALY VIA WIKIMEDIA COMMONS)

RIGHT: A battery of Italian Ansaldo 149/40 M1935 guns prepare to fire in North Africa. (EUROPEAN UNION ASALDO VIA WIKIMEDIA COMMONS)

BELOW: The Ansaldo 149/40 M1935 was intended to replace the Cannone da 149/35A pictured here during World War One. (CREATIVE COMMONS ITALIAN ARMY PHOTOGRAPHERS OF 1915-1918 VIA WIKIMEDIA COMMONS)

Although few of the Italian heavy Ansaldo 149/40 M1935s were actually completed, the big gun had been intended to replace the elderly Cannone da 149/35A as Benito Mussolini embarked on a campaign of conquest and joined the Axis forces in World War Two. While an order for 590 had been specified by 1940, only about 50 were delivered by the Ansaldo company of Genoa.

The 149.1mm gun fired a high explosive shell that weighed just over 100lb to a maximum range of nearly 26,000 yards. Its barrel stretched 20ft, 10in, and the system displaced 25,000lb. The gun utilised the Welin screw breech with hydropneumatic recoil. Its size required that it be moved in two parts and reassembled in the field. For use in more difficult terrain, it could be further broken down into four pieces. Its efficiency was impeded

by the use of trail spades that were hammered into the ground to assist in the absorption of recoil. The weapon was emplaced atop a split trail carriage and was transported by Breda trucks.

The Ansaldo 149/40 entered service with the Italian Army in 1940 and proved to be a significant improvement in firepower over earlier models. However, its lack of mobility and relative scarcity on the battlefield prevented it from completely replacing obsolete types. The towed version of the weapon was later developed into the tracked Semovente 149/40 self-propelled gun, which was used as a mobile heavy weapon providing indirect fire with the gun mounted to a tank chassis.

After the Italian surrender of 1943, some Ansaldo 149/40 models fell into German hands. For the remainder of World War Two, these were pressed into service as the 150mm K 408(i).

Ansaldo 149/40 M1935	
Country of Origin	Italy
Calibre	149.1mm
Crew	12
Range	25,900 yards
Rate of Fire	2 rounds per minute
Number manufactured	51

Howitzers

Mainstay in Field and Siege

By the mid-20th Century, the origin of the howitzer dated back more than 600 years. Its effectiveness and versatility in the field were regularly demonstrated, and howitzers fulfilled multiple roles in offensive and defensive land warfare.

The howitzer is generally defined as a field artillery weapon that bridged the gap between the routinely level firing field gun and the high-angle fire of the mortar. Therefore, they were constructed with a shorter barrel than field guns and an arc of fire that allowed their shells to plunge toward the target. The advantage in plunging indirect fire lay in the ability of the howitzer to hit enemy positions that were sometimes hidden behind hills or other geographic features and out of sight. The howitzer's higher angle of fire was also effective against fortified enemy positions, such as bunkers or pillboxes. The penetrating capability of their rounds was often more capable of destroying a hardened target than that of the flat-firing field gun.

Howitzers were produced in great numbers by the major adversaries during World War Two. They were particularly well suited to infantry support in indirect fire, direct fire, counter battery fire and even the anti-tank role when desperate situations emerged. During the inter-war years, a movement to develop an even more versatile field artillery weapon sought to combine the best attributes of both the howitzer and the field gun. One of the best examples of the successful marriage of these was the British 25-pounder, which over time replaced both the 18-pounder field gun and the 4.5-inch howitzer of World War One.

Among the most common howitzers employed during World War Two were the British 25-pounder, along with legacy examples of the 4.5-inch weapon, the German 105mm leFH18 and 155mm sFH, the Soviet 122mm M1938 (M30) and 152mm gun-howitzer M1937 (ML20) and the American M2A1 105mm, M3 105mm and M1 155mm. These weapons became legendary for their impact on the outcome of land campaigns in World War Two.

ABOVE: The Ordnance QF 25-pounder became a prime example of the gun howitzer concept. (CREATIVE COMMONS AUSTRALIAN WAR MEMORIAL BUKVOED VIA WIKIMEDIA COMMONS)

LEFT: An American factory worker removes the barrel of a 105mm howitzer from a boring machine on the floor of a facility in Milwaukee, Wisconsin. (LIBRARY OF CONGRESS VIA WIKIMEDIA COMMONS)

LEFT: US Marines fire a 155mm howitzer against Japanese positions on the island of Iwo Jima. (CREATIVE COMMONS USMC HISTORY DIVISION ARCHIVES BRANCH VIA WIKIMEDIA COMMONS)

M1 Pack 75mm

Steady amid Rugged Terrain

ABOVE: British soldiers of the 1st Airlanding Light Artillery Regiment service their 75mm pack howitzer in Italy. (COLLECTIONS OF THE IMPERIAL WAR MUSEUMS VIA WIKIMEDIA COMMONS)

RIGHT: A US Marine crew fires a 75mm pack howitzer in action on the island of Tinian in the Marianas. (US MARINE CORPS VIA WIKIMEDIA COMMONS)

Artillery has always provided a distinct advantage in fighting through difficult terrain, as long as the piece could be transported, assembled and made combat-worthy. This ability was addressed by the US Army between the world wars, and the solution took the form of the M1 Pack 75mm howitzer.

The gun provided powerful punch for its size and, to facilitate its use in the field, it was capable of being broken down into multiple loads and could be parachuted into action for use with light infantry or airborne troops. It was carried overland in either seven loads on the backs of pack animals, dropped in nine parachute loads or carried by four soldiers. It was also transportable in tow and fully assembled by a ¾-tonne truck.

Development of the M1 Pack howitzer began in 1920 and proceeded slowly, with the standardisation of the weapon occurring in the summer of 1927. Inter-war funding restrictions prevented large-scale production, so only 32 had been completed by 1932. Even as war in Europe broke out, only 91 were in service in 1940, but production ramped up substantially and the M1 Pack became a mainstay of the Allied forces. The howitzer weighed 1,439lb, its barrel was 4ft, 6in long and it operated from a box or split trail carriage with a horizontal block breech and hydropneumatic constant recoil mechanism. A second variant, the M1A1, entered production with a modified breech block and breech ring soon after mass production got underway in September 1940. Production continued through the end of 1944.

During World War Two, the US Marine Corps and US Army, particularly in airborne divisions, fielded the 75mm Pack howitzer extensively. Its range of 5½ miles, steady rate of fire, and versatility in both offense and defence were often critical in battle. The weapon rendered great service in the Pacific during heavy fighting on the islands of Guadalcanal, Tarawa and Saipan. In western Europe and Italy it performed well under extreme conditions. Its use only began to diminish when the 105mm howitzer became available in quantity.

The M1 75mm Pack howitzer was the second most common weapon of its type to serve in World War Two. After 1962, it was designated the M116 and examples remain in service around the world today.

RIGHT: A pair of M1 75mm howitzers on outdoor display at a museum in Taiwan. (CREATIVE COMMONS 玄史生 VIA WIKIMEDIA COMMONS)

M1 Pack 75mm	
Country of Origin	United States
Calibre	75mm
Crew	6
Range	5½ miles
Rate of Fire	6 rounds per minute
Number manufactured	8,400

M2 105mm

Versatility in the Field

The M2 105mm was the primary field howitzer of the US ground forces during World War Two.

During the inter-war years, the army had recognised its shortcomings both in available artillery and its use on the battlefield. Captured German 105mm howitzers were thoroughly evaluated during the programme of improvement. Designated in numerous variants based on structural improvements and carriage modifications, the M2 was a versatile light field howitzer whose first iteration appeared in 1920 as the M1920 mounted on Carriage M1920. Accepted for production in late 1927, the 105mm was intended to replace existing 75mm howitzers and field guns. However, limited funding restricted production into the next decade and, by 1933, only 14 howitzers had been completed.

The original M1 105mm was modified in the early 1930s and redesignated the M2. The howitzer weighed 4,980lb, its barrel length was 7ft, 7in, and it fired via a horizontal block breech and hydropneumatic recoil system primarily from a split trail carriage. It was relatively heavy for a field howitzer, but it was transportable in tow and provided accurate sustained fire at a moderate range. The weight was determined to be a reasonable trade-off for durability in the field, although extensive action did eventually cause cracks to develop in the muzzle. This issue was addressed with an additional step in the manufacturing process after World War Two.

The primary task of the 105mm howitzer was to break up enemy troop concentrations and provide direct support. However, its elevation and traverse made it effective in indirect firing missions as well. It gained a positive reputation with the first deployments of US ground troops to North Africa in 1942. Its widespread use included action in western Europe from D-Day through the Battle of the Bulge and victory in Europe, as well as island fighting in the Pacific, where it was prominent at Iwo Jima, Okinawa and elsewhere. Numerous other Allied nations fielded the M2 and, by the end of World War Two, more than 8,500 had been manufactured.

The M2 continued in production through 1953 and was deployed in later conflicts of the 20th Century. Redesignated the M101 in 1960, it remains in service in some countries.

ABOVE: French artillerymen receive instruction on the M2 105mm howitzer in Morocco, December 1943. (US ARMY VIA WIKIMEDIA COMMONS)

LEFT: A 2½-ton truck tows an M2 105mm howitzer along a beach en route to the Algerian desert. (LIBRARY OF CONGRESS VIA WIKIMEDIA COMMONS)

BELOW: This M2 105mm howitzer resides at Batey ha-Osef military museum in Israel. (CREATIVE COMMONS BUKVOED VIA WIKIMEDIA COMMONS)

M2 105mm	
Country of Origin	United States
Calibre	105mm
Crew	8
Range	12,300 yards
Rate of Fire	10 rounds per minute maximum
Number manufactured	10,200

M1 155mm 'Long Tom'

Instrumental Across the Globe

RIGHT: This M1 155mm howitzer is on display at the US Army Field Artillery Museum, Fort Sill, Oklahoma. (CREATIVE COMMONS STURMVOGEL 66 VIA WIKIMEDIA COMMONS)

RIGHT: This M114 howitzer has been moved into firing position during exercises in the 1980s. (US ARMY VIA WIKIMEDIA COMMONS)

BELOW: The earliest iteration of the eventual M1 155mm howitzer was this Model 1920. (US ARMY VIA WIKIMEDIA COMMONS)

Although they shared a historic nickname, 'Long Tom,', and generally utilised the same carriage, the M1 155mm gun and M1 155mm howitzer were distinctly different weapons, their battlefield roles divided based on capabilities.

A significant component of the post-World War One modernisation of US Army artillery, the M1 155mm howitzer was intended to supplant the existing French Schneider Modele 1917, which had been relied on during World War One. The army commitment to the 155mm howitzer was affirmed in 1929 with particular emphasis on rapid towing capability by truck. However, difficulties with the construction of a suitable carriage delayed development and two new carriages were tested for use. The howitzer was put through trials in the early 1930s, but the programme failed to gain traction until the end of the decade. In 1937, further testing took place and, within the year, further study of European howitzers confirmed the need for a heavier weapon than the existing 755mm and 105mm.

The M1 155mm entered production after acceptance by the army in the spring of 1941. It weighed 12,800lb while under tow, operated with a split trail carriage and fired with a slow-cone interrupted screw breech. Its barrel stretched 12ft, 5in and allowed the howitzer to fire a nearly 95-pound shell a distance of 16,000 yards. The barrel was manufactured at the Watervliet Arsenal in New York, while the recoil mechanism and gun carriage were built at the Rock Island Arsenal in Illinois.

The M1 155mm renamed M114 after World War Two, was instrumental in Allied ground operations across the globe. The weapon was first in action with the 34th Field Artillery Battalion in North Africa in 1942 and in Italy, western Europe and the Pacific. It earned a reputation for outstanding accuracy and was beloved by artillerymen. Many of them attested to the fact that it was "the sweetest weapon on the front."

After World War Two, the howitzer was renamed the M114 and was widely exported to other nations. Although production ended in 1953, it remains in service in some countries to this day.

M1 155mm 'Long Tom'	
Country of Origin	United States
Calibre	155mm
Crew	14
Range	16,000 yards
Rate of Fire	4 rounds per minute
Number manufactured	10,300

M3 Light

An Airborne Augmentation

As the growth of airborne formations, including parachute and glider troops, gained momentum in the US Army prior to the nation's entry into World War Two, the requirement for artillery support that was light, mobile and transportable by air increased. This situation gave rise to the 105mm M3 Light howitzer, which essentially combined the standard 105mm with a shortened barrel to the recoil system and the split trail carriage of the 75mm Pack howitzer.

Research began in 1941 and the prototype was tested at Aberdeen Proving Ground in Maryland in March 1942. Its barrel had been shortened by 27in to 6ft, 2in, and the entire assembly weighed 2,495lb. The M3 howitzer fired the same ammunition as the standard 105mm, but the shortened barrel led to the requirement for a modified propellant consisting of a base charge with the introduction of up to four additional increments. These were made with faster burning powder to reduce the frequency of incomplete burning. Such was a trade-off as the range of the M3 was reduced from that of the

ABOVE: This 105mm M3 Light howitzer is displayed outdoors at the Army Museum in Honolulu, Hawaii. (PUBLIC DOMAIN MAX SMITH VIA WIKIMEDIA COMMONS)

LEFT: American troops unload an M3 Light howitzer in New Guinea. (GOVERNMENT OF AUSTRALIA VIA WIKIMEDIA COMMONS)

standard howitzer. Just after trials, the original carriage was succeeded by the modified carriage M3A1, which included trails of thicker steel.

The M3 Light howitzer entered production in February 1943 and proceeded through May 1944. Following a brief interruption, more were manufactured from April to June 1945, becoming organic to the airborne table of organisation and equipment (TO&E).

The M3 was deployed to airborne units of the US Army to augment the numbers of existing 75mm Pack howitzers in the early spring of 1944, and it saw service from D-day forward in western Europe after being airlifted for service with glider field artillery battalions in Normandy. In the beginning, a single 105mm battalion joined the three 75mm howitzer battalions that were standard. This was expanded later with a total of four

glider field artillery battalions, one of them utilising the M3. On the ground, the weapon was transportable in tow by the 1/4-tonne jeep or the 1½-tonne truck. British, French and Latin American troops used the M3 in small numbers.

BELOW: Artillerymen probably attached to the US 4th Infantry Division operate an M3 light howitzer in France, 1944. (CREATIVE COMMONS PHOTOSNORMANDIE VIA WIKIMEDIA COMMONS)

M3 Light	
Country of Origin	United States
Calibre	105mm
Crew	10
Range	8,300 yards
Rate of Fire	2 rounds per minute
Number manufactured	2,580

M1 240mm

The Powerful Black Dragon

RIGHT: M1 240mm emplaced beneath camouflage netting in Italy in 1944. (NATIONAL ARCHIVES AND RECORDS ADMINISTRATION VIA WIKIMEDIA COMMONS)

Nicknamed the 'Black Dragon' by its crews, the M1 240mm howitzer's bore was equivalent to 9.45in and was the heaviest field artillery weapon of the US Army during World War Two. It shared a carriage with the M1 203mm M1 field gun, but was developed for different firing missions.

During World War One, America had procured the French Mortier de 280 Modele 1914 manufactured by Schneider and built the howitzer under license as the M1918. However, an improved design effort was undertaken in the mid-1920s and progress was quite slow, with funding constraints and lack of support throttling the programme. Then, in the spring of 1940, the effort to replace the M1918 was revived to produce a howitzer that was capable of delivering heavy fire against fortified enemy positions from long range.

RIGHT: An M1 240mm in action in December 1944 during the Allied drive into Germany. (US ARMY SIGNAL CORPS VIA WIKIMEDIA COMMONS)

Production of the new M1 240mm began in November 1942. The big howitzer weighed 64,700lb, while its barrel was 27ft, 6in long and it operated with an interrupted screw breech, hydropneumatic recoil and split trail carriage. Ground transport was accomplished in two pieces, with the barrel and carriage loaded on six-wheeled wagons developed specifically for the task. The original transport truck was deemed inadequate for difficult or muddy terrain, so the tracked M6 tractor was developed for it.

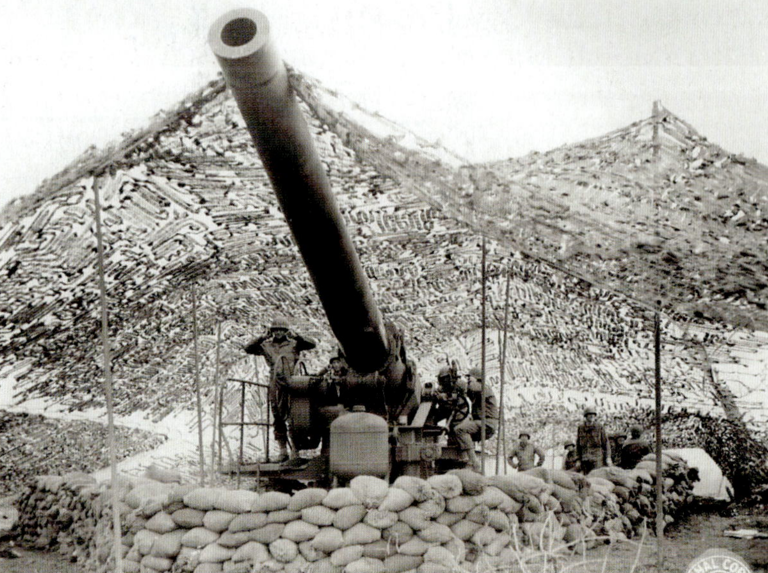

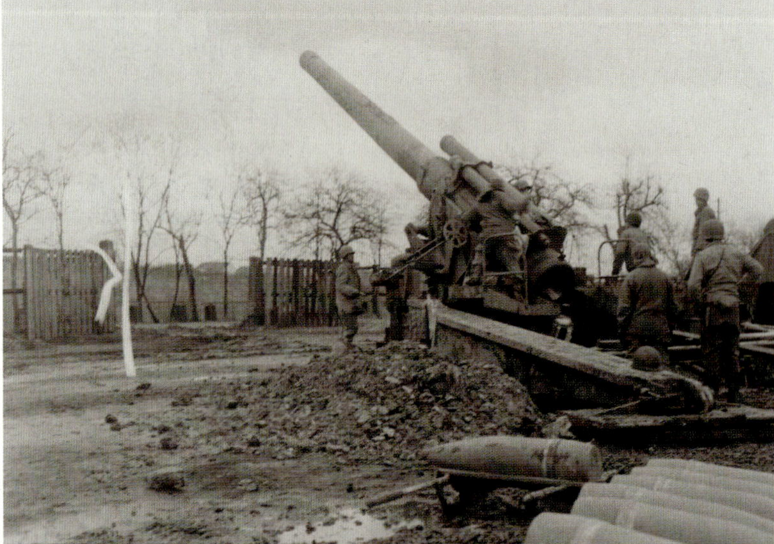

M1 240mm	
Country of Origin	United States
Calibre	240mm (9.45 inches)
Crew	14
Range	14.3 miles
Rate of Fire	1 round per minute
Number manufactured	315

The M1 240mm was first used in combat at the Anzio beachhead in Italy in January 1944, when the 697th and 698th Field Artillery Battalions shelled German positions. In action, the accuracy of the weapon proved to be less than ideal, while sustained firing over lengthy periods resulted in excessive bore wear. Nevertheless, the howitzer was further utilised in action around Monte Cassino.

All 240mm units were transferred to western Europe by late 1944, and the howitzer went into action against the Siegfried Line on the German frontier. Some reports contradicted the reputation of the M3 for inaccuracy with comments praising its "devastating firepower and incredible accuracy." Certainly, in some cases, its power was decisive. The weapon was also notably used in the Pacific during the battle against the Japanese for control of Manila, capital city of the Philippines.

The M1 240mm remained in service during the Korean War, with many transferred to the armed forces of Taiwan in the late 1950s.

BELOW: The sheer size of the M1 howitzer's breech is apparent in this example at Fort Sill, Oklahoma. (CREATIVE COMMONS JASON LONG VIA WIKIMEDIA COMMONS)

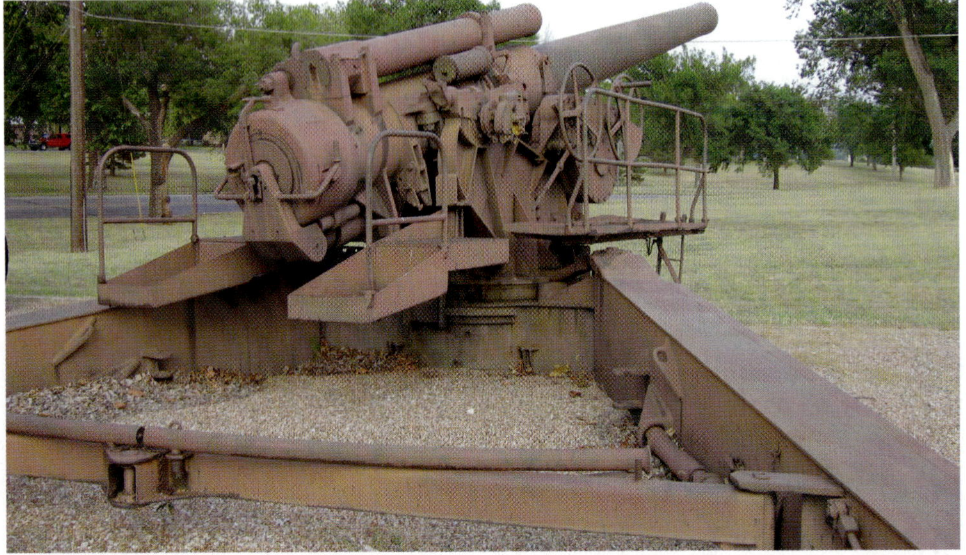

leFH 18M Light

The leFH 18M Light howitzer was an improved version of the standard field howitzer of the German Army in World War Two. Its design emerged in the late 1920s with the leFH 18, with performance that exceeded the earlier World War One-vintage leFH 16.

The 105mm leFH 18M was actually quite similar to the original leFH 18, which entered service with the Wehrmacht in 1935. The early leFH 18 was conceived in response to a covert order from the Army Ordnance Office that was issued in 1927, and it was found that the 105mm weapon was substantially more effective in trials than existing 75mm howitzers while additional expense was minimal.

Production of the leFH 18 began in the early 1930s and, by the eve of World War Two, nearly 4,900 were in service with the German Army. Manufacturing continued through the war and, by 1945, the number reached nearly 7,000. Original wood-spoked wheels for the split trail carriage were replaced with cast metal in 1936, and rubber tyres made the howitzer more mobile in the field. Although it was intended to be horse-drawn or towed, its substantial weight of 7,690lb made vehicle towing by prime mover the preferred method. The howitzer was operated with a horizontal sliding block breech with hydropneumatic recoil.

By 1941, the German arms manufacturer Rheinmetall had undertaken efforts to modify the leFH 18 to gain better range. This effort was successful, eclipsing the range of the early leFH 18 of 11,674 yards by more than 1,800 yards. The leFH 18M supplanted its predecessor as the primary Wehrmacht field howitzer as World War Two progressed. The primary distinction between the two was the addition of a muzzle brake to the 9ft, 8in barrel that allowed for heavier propellant charges and greater range. The versatility of the basic weapon was enhanced, and the leFH 18M entered full production in 1941, being deployed in action that same year.

The leFH 18 and follow-on leFH 18M were both commonly used by Wehrmacht formations throughout World War Two in North Africa, Italy and the Eastern and Western Fronts.

ABOVE: A German soldier works to position an leFH 105mm howitzer in December 1943. (CREATIVE COMMONS BUNDESARCHIV BILD VIA WIKIMEDIA COMMONS)

LEFT: Artillerymen fire an leFH 105mm howitzer in the heat of action on the Eastern Front. (CREATIVE COMMONS BUNDESARCHIV BILD VIA WIKIMEDIA COMMONS)

leFH 18 & 18M Light Howitzer	
Country of Origin	Germany
Calibre	105mm
Crew	6
Range	11,674 yards; 13,479 yards
Rate of Fire	6 rounds per minute
Number manufactured	11,795

LEFT: This leFH 18 105mm Howitzer, manufactured before or during World War Two, is now in a museum in Poland. (CREATIVE COMMONS ZALA VIA WIKIMEDIA COMMONS)

leFH 18/40 Light

Worthy but Weighty

The leFH 18 and 18M Light howitzers that were common to Wehrmacht ground formations during World War Two performed well in the field. However, one drawback was their weight, which impacted mobility and rapid deployment. In an effort to increase rapid movement, the German military establishment issued a directive to produce a lighter field howitzer in the spring of 1942. The order came with some urgency as the German military had begun to experience setbacks on the battlefield as resistance stiffened in North Africa and on the Eastern Front. The renewed research produced a combination that became quite efficient in the field artillery role.

The LeFH 18/40 Light howitzer was the product of the proven leFH18M barrel, with a double-baffled muzzle brake and the carriage of the 75mm Pak 40 anti-tank gun. The two-wheel split trail carriage employed long torsion bars to support the wheels, which replaced the original carriage's wooden wheels in large steel configuration with rubber tyres. The barrel was 9ft, 8in long and recoil was hydropneumatic. The howitzer weighed 4,311lb. Production time improved with the modifications and thousands of the leFH 18/40 were fielded in the final three years of World War Two.

Designated '18' in reference to 1918, the earliest year of leFH development, and '40' in reference to the carriage of the Pak 40, the leFH 18/40 was indeed lighter and could be towed more easily by vehicles such as the Opel Blitz medium duty truck or SdKfz 251 half-track armoured personnel carrier.

The leFH 18/40 entered service in 1942 and took its place alongside its predecessors as the standard light howitzer of the Wehrmacht and Waffen SS for the duration of World War Two. It was deployed on all fronts and was found particularly useful in the East, where a war of movement often ensued following the seizure of the initiative by the Red Army by 1943. Its versatility, mobility, superior firepower to 75mm howitzers and rate of fire were among the best in service.

leFH 18/40 Light Howitzer	
Country of Origin	Germany
Calibre	105mm
Crew	6
Range	13,479 yards
Rate of Fire	6 rounds per minute
Number manufactured	10,265

The standard German heavy field howitzer at the division level throughout World War Two, the sFH 18 was nicknamed 'Evergreen' by its crews and was a ubiquitous presence on all fronts. The weapon was common in field artillery battalions and was noted for its mobility and firepower.

Manufactured by Krupp, Rheinmetall, Spreewerke, MAN and the Czech Skoda works, the sFH 18 was developed to replace the World War One-era 150mm sFH 13, which was heavily scrutinised in post-war circles. The new design provided marked improvements in overall performance. Although it was twice as heavy as the older howitzer at 13,898lb, it delivered substantially greater muzzle velocity and improved range, hurling a 97-pound shell well over

sFH 18 Howitzer 150mm	
Country of Origin	Germany
Calibre	150mm
Crew	12
Range	10,660 yards
Rate of Fire	4 rounds per minute
Number manufactured	6,756

sFH 18 150mm

The Wehrmacht's Evergreen

10,000 yards, while its innovative split trail carriage allowed substantially greater traverse. Covert design work was undertaken in 1926, flouting the terms of the Versailles Treaty, with the German arms manufacturers building a production model by 1933.

Along with the 150mm Kanone 18 and the short-barrelled infantry gun sIG 33, the sFH 18 was one of three 150mm field artillery pieces deployed by German ground forces in World War Two. Its carriage was the same as the Kanone 18, with a split trail design, box legs and spades that could be mounted on the legs for increased stability of the firing platform. The howitzer was designed for horse transport, while motorised transportation came along later. The weapon was broken down into two loads with the former and transported in a single load with the latter.

The sFH 18 officially entered service in May 1935, weeks after Adolf Hitler repudiated the Versailles Treaty and announced to the world that Germany was rearming. Its initial combat use occurred with Chinese forces during the Second Sino-Japanese War. Despite its enhanced performance, the sFH 18's range was inferior to some Soviet guns on the Eastern Front. Range was boosted with rocket-assisted ammunition, and experimentation with a barrel that was longer than the standard 14ft, 7in proved disappointing as it lessened accuracy.

Military analysts have assessed the performance of the sFH 18 and determined it was one of the most important German ground weapons of World War Two.

ABOVE: This example of the sFH Howitzer 150mm is located outdoors at the Svidnik War Museum in Slovakia. (SVIDNIK WAR MUSEUM VIA WIKIMEDIA COMMONS)

LEFT: This sFH 18 150mm howitzer is show with crew preparing for action at Kursk on the Eastern Front. (CREATIVE COMMONS BUNDESARCHIV BILD VIA WIKIMEDIA COMMONS)

LEFT: Shown at the Base Borden Military Museum in Ontario, Canada, the sFH Howitzer 150mm remains an imposing weapon. (CREATIVE COMMONS BALCER-COMMONSWIKI VIA WIKIMEDIA COMMONS)

M1937 & M1938 152mm; M1938 122mm

Soviet Next Generation Hardware

RIGHT: These M1937 ML-20 gun howitzers reside in a museum in St. Petersburg, Russia. (CREATIVE COMMONS MATTHIASKABEL VIA WIKIMEDIA COMMONS)

RIGHT: Soviet artillerymen fire the M-30 122mm howitzer during offensive operations in 1944. (GOVERNMENT OF UKRAINE VIA WIKIMEDIA COMMON)

During the inter-war years, the Soviet military establishment grappled with the perceived shortcomings of its artillery deployed in 1914-1917 and its defeat at the hands of Imperial Germany. Recognising the need for a new generation of field artillery, its howitzer research and development gained new impetus and produced a suite of effective weapons in the Model 1937 152mm gun-howitzer ML-20, the Model 1938 152mm howitzer M-10 and the Model 1938 122mm howitzer M-30.

Leading the effort to produce the field howitzers that resulted in heavy concentrations of Red Army artillery fire across the Eastern Front in World War Two was the eminent design engineer FF Petrov, who headed the design bureau of Motovilikha, also known as Plant No 172. Each of these new designs came to fruition in the 1930s, with serial production of the ML-20 undertaken in 1937 and the M-10 and M-30 following two years later.

The ML-20 was developed as a gun howitzer, exhibiting the characteristics of both high trajectory fire and more direct fire in combat situations. A substantial upgrade from the earlier 152mm gun M1910/34, the ML-20 was a corps and army level weapon that was highly successful in its designated roles and rendered distinguished service with the Red Army through the drive to Berlin. It weighed 16,027lb with a barrel length of 13ft, 11in, interrupted screw breech, split trail carriage, and

hydropneumatic recoil. Produced through 1946, its first combat experience was during the Battle of Khalkin Gol, during border clashes with the Japanese in Manchuria. Its reliability in the field, ease of maintenance and effectiveness in the dual role of gun howitzer resulted in a long service life.

The 152mm M-10 was developed concurrently with the ML-20, but the overarching mission of this weapon differed slightly. Intended as a dedicated howitzer, the M-10 was built with a short barrel of 11ft, 7in and was mounted on a split trail carriage that was transportable by ZiS-5 truck. Its focus on indirect fire and medium range were complementary to other field artillery in the Red Army table of organisation and equipment.

The M-30 122mm served as a light field weapon and was the standard howitzer of the Red Army at the divisional and army group levels. Reliable and versatile, it fired effective high-explosive and armour-piercing rounds. Its split trail carriage was an adequate firing platform, while the interrupted screw breech and hydropneumatic recoil were key to its effective rate of fire. The M-30 weighed 5,401lb and was transportable by horse or vehicles, which achieved road speeds of more than 30 miles per hour with the howitzer in tow.

Produced in great numbers, the M-30 was one of the most successful field howitzers of World War Two, tough and reliable in action. It became the backbone of the Red Army artillery during the Great Patriotic War.

M1937 & M1938 152mm; M1938 122mm	
Country of Origin	Soviet Union
Calibre	152mm and 122mm
Crew	6; 10; 8
Range	10.7 miles; 7.33 miles; 7.7 miles
Rate of Fire	4, 4 and 6 rounds per minute
Number manufactured	6,884; 1,522; 19,266

RIGHT: The open breech of an M-10 152mm howitzer awaits a shell loaded by Finnish soldiers. (GOVERNMENT OF FINLAND VIA WIKIMEDIA COMMONS)

Type 92 Light

Accepted into service with the Imperial Japanese Army in 1932, the Type 92 Light howitzer, also known as the Type 92 Battalion Gun, was well liked among the artillerymen who serviced it through the Second Sino-Japanese War and World War Two.

Classified as a field howitzer, the weapon was in fact capable of both indirect fire and direct fire in ground support, so it can also be considered a gun howitzer in the trend of the times with armament requirements. The smaller calibre Type 11 37mm infantry gun and Type 11 70mm infantry mortar had been deemed below expectations in early testing and combat, and the initiative to develop the 70mm Type 92 also arose to simplify the supply chain that otherwise required troops to carry two types of ammunition into battle.

Under the requirements issued by the Army Technical Design Bureau, the Type 92 was a light, stubby weapon that weighed 476lb with a short barrel of just 2ft, 4in length, with a split trail carriage. It operated with an interrupted thread drop breechblock and hydro-spring recoil. Originally built with large wooden wheels, the carriage was later modified with steel wheels with large holes punched in. The Type 92 was easily disassembled and designed to be transported by a team of three horses. In extreme situations the

Type 92 Light Howitzer	
Country of Origin	Japan
Calibre	70mm
Crew	5
Range	3,060 yards
Rate of Fire	10 rounds per minute
Number manufactured	2,876

weapon was often pulled by a single animal. Its elevation was from near vertical to horizontal with a hand crank, and the size of the weapon made it movable by the soldiers themselves if necessary.

The Type 92 was versatile in the field and, at close range, was effective against the armour of American M4 Sherman medium tanks. It first saw action against Chinese forces on the Asian continent and against the Soviet Red Army during the Battle of Khalkhin Gol during the 1939 border clashes in Manchuria. It was deployed extensively with Japanese troops in defence of occupied islands across the Pacific during World War Two and remained in service for at least three decades afterward in the hands of Indonesian, Korean and Vietnamese forces.

TOP: Japanese soldiers operate a Type 92 Light howitzer in the field. (GOVERNMENT OF CHINA VIA WIKIMEDIA COMMONS)

ABOVE: The high trajectory of the Japanese Type 92 Light howitzer is displayed with this example at Fort Sill, Oklahoma. (CREATIVE COMMONS STURMVOGEL 66 VIA WIKIMEDIA COMMONS)

LEFT: US Marines fire a captured Type 92 Light howitzer captured on the island of Saipan in 1944. (NATIONAL ARCHIVES AND RECORDS ADMINISTRATION VIA WIKIMEDIA COMMONS)

Canon de 105 Court mle 1934 Schneider

Limited Deployment by 1940

Indicative of the product line developed and manufactured by Schneider et Cie during World War One and the inter-war years, the Canon de 105 court mle 1934 was intended for use by the French armed forces after a similar model had been sold to the Japanese.

The mle 1934 weighed 3,796lb, employed a horizontal sliding block breech with a gun barrel of 6ft, 10in length, and utilised a hydropneumatic recoil system with split trail carriage. The carriage was of steel wheel construction and the wheels actually moved with the trail legs as the weapon was deployed into firing position, providing an enhanced stability to the firing platform with a 'toe in' emplacement.

Production of the mle 1934 was quite limited, from 1935 through 1938, and 70 of these were sold to Lithuania in 1937, proving a commercial aspect to the type. Late

Canon de 105 court mle 1934 Schneider	
Country of Origin	France
Calibre	105mm
Crew	7
Range	11,700 yards
Rate of Fire	5 rounds per minute
Number manufactured	144

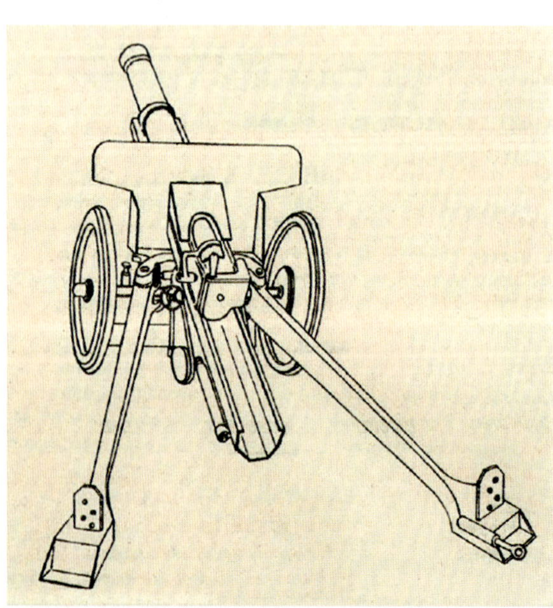

in 1939, the Turkish Army acquired a dozen mle 1934s from France. When the Battle of France erupted in 1940, only a relative few were in service with French forces. Sources relate that a mere 60 examples had been deployed with the 1st Armoured and 3rd Motorised Divisions. The Germans took captured examples and placed them in service, renamed the 105mm leFH 324(f).

The mle 1934 fired a 35-pound shell to a maximum range of 11,700 yards, but even as its entered production a replacement was being developed. The Canon de 105 court mle 1935B was a product of the French State Arsenal at Bourges. Another traditional design, it elicited an order from the French Army for more than 610 of them, which were considered an improvement over the mle 1934. However, only about 230 had been accepted into service before the fateful spring of 1940. When Italian forces occupied southern France in concert with the German conquest of France and the Low Countries, they captured 127 examples of the mle 1935B and placed them in service as the Obice da 105/15.

BL 7.2-inch

Howitzer Old is New Again

BL 7.2-Inch Howitzer	
Country of Origin	Great Britain
Calibre	183mm
Crew	12
Range	19,667 yards (Mk 6)
Rate of Fire	3 rounds per minute
Number manufactured	78

In 1940, with World War Two raging, the British Army became concerned that the performance of its World War One stalwart, the BL 8-Inch howitzer, was inadequate for the demands of a modern war. The BL 8-Inch had been deployed liberally during the previous conflict, but its range had to be improved to provide heavy infantry fire support. The immediate solution was the re-lining of the existing tubes to a slightly smaller calibre and the introduction of a new series of ammunition to achieve the desired range. The early BL 7.2-Inch howitzers used during World War Two were an outgrowth of the older weapon rather than a completely new system. The 'BL' designation remained, denoting breech-loading rather than muzzle-loading operations.

The BL 7.2-Inch was developed from the summer of 1940 in 183mm rather than 203mm, as its predecessor had been manufactured. The new howitzer fired a 200-pound shell 16,900 yards and utilised the familiar Welin Screw and Asbury breech firing mechanism with slight modifications and a new barrel of 14ft, 3in in length. It weighed 20,760lb and utilised the same box trail carriage with its steel rimmed wheels eventually modified with pneumatic tyres

as the British Army became more thoroughly mechanised. Its recoil included a hydraulic buffer and hydropneumatic recuperator. It was originally towed cross country by the Scammell Pioneer R100 gun tractor and then the Albion CX22S.

The BL-7.2 entered service with artillery batteries in North Africa in 1942 and was fielded throughout the campaign in western Europe after D-Day in 1944. It was in action throughout the remainder of World War Two, regularly deployed in regiments of the Army Group Royal Artillery that included two batteries of four guns teamed with a pair of four-gun batteries of the 155mm 'Long Tom' howitzer.

Production continued into 1944 and a total of six marks with additional sub-variants were built. The Mk I was converted to the carriage MI of the US 'Long Tom', which resulted in the Mk V designation. One challenge in the field emerged with the substantial recoil generated with the new ammunition, which caused the gun to lurch violently backward. In 1943, adjustments to the carriage were initiated to address this issue, along with a lengthened barrel to produce the Mk 6, which exhibited longer range as well.

QF 4.5-inch

Mobility Lesson Learned

The origin of the QF 4.5-inch howitzer stretched back half-a-century and through desperate combat by the time World War Two broke out in 1939. The weapon was the product of the British experience during the Boer War, when it was discovered – much to the chagrin of officer and soldier alike – that existing field artillery types were too heavy for mobile combat across the tracts of southern Africa. In response, an equipment committee convened in 1901 and, after a competition, recommended the design submission for the 114.3mm howitzer from Coventry Ordnance Works for procurement.

Testing occurred in 1906 and, by 1908, the original barrel was shortened for production. The QF (quick firing) 4.5-inch howitzer replaced the older BL 5-inch howitzer and was extensively in service by 1910. It became the standard light field howitzer of the British Army and Commonwealth forces in World War One, equipping about one quarter of the army's field artillery units.

The 4.5-inch howitzer weighed 3,010lb with a horizontal sliding breech block with hydro-spring recoil and sturdy box trail carriage. Its barrel length stretched 5ft, 10in and it was transported by teams of six or eight horses, although later modifications allowed towing by motorised vehicles. The howitzer was produced in multiple marks before production ceased in 1944, and it fired a 35-pound high explosive shell an effective range of 6,600 yards. By the end of World War One, an estimated 3,177 4.5-inch howitzers had been manufactured.

With the outbreak of World War Two, the British deployed those 4.5-inch weapons that had been retained in service through the inter-war years. Improvements to the earlier marks included replacing the wooden carriage wheels with pneumatic tyres. The British Expeditionary Force landed in France with the howitzer as a primary field artillery piece, while Australian, New Zealand, Canadian and South African forces also operated the 4.5-inch, as well as numerous other countries.

During the 1940 debacle in France, a reported 96 4.5-inch howitzers were lost in action, some of them captured by the Germans and put in service as the 114mm leFH 361(e). The model also served in the early months of World War Two in North Africa, in the Levant and notably in the fighting along the Malayan peninsula and at Hong Kong against the Japanese.

As the war progressed, the QF 4.5-inch howitzer was gradually replaced by the 25-pounder gun beginning in 1943.

RIGHT: New Zealanders are shown with their QF 4.5-inch Howitzer in 1940. (COLLECTIONS OF THE IMPERIAL WAR MUSEUMS VIA WIKIMEDIA COMMONS)

RIGHT: Australian gunners fire the QF 4.5-inch Howitzer in exercises in 1935. (GOVERNMENT OF AUSTRALIA VIA WIKIMEDIA COMMONS)

RIGHT: Camouflaged QF 4.5-inch howitzers near the French town of Arras in the spring of 1917. (COLLECTIONS OF THE IMPERIAL WAR MUSEUMS VIA WIKIMEDIA COMMONS)

QF 4.5-Inch Howitzer	
Country of Origin	Great Britain
Calibre	4.5-inch (114.3mm)
Crew	6
Range	6,600 yards
Rate of Fire	4 rounds per minute
Number manufactured	3,359

Obice M75/18 Modello 34

A Light Mountain Weapon

Designed by Ansaldo, the Obice M75/18 modello 34 was a 75mm howitzer initially developed as a light mountain artillery piece. It was conceived by Lieutenant Colonel Sergio Berlese, an officer of the Italian Army, and entered production in 1934. Soon afterward, the modello 34 was adapted into the standard light infantry howitzer designated modello 35.

There were marked differences between the two variants. The modello 34 could be disassembled into eight components for transport across rough terrain, while the modello 35 remained intact during movement. While the modello 34 was built with a box trail carriage, the modello 35 was of split trail carriage. Each howitzer had a barrel length of 5ft, 1.3in, and operated with a horizontal sliding wedge breech and hydropneumatic recoil system. Both howitzers fired a 14.2-pound shell a distance of nearly 10,500 yards, somewhat shorter than other contemporary Italian artillery pieces.

The modello 1934 was deployed in combat for the first time during the Spanish Civil War of the mid-1930s and was later used in Greece, the Balkans, North Africa, Italy and France. Following the Axis invasion of the Soviet Union in 1941, the modello 35 saw its primary combat use on the Eastern Front. The modello 35 was also built for the export market during the inter-war years and was sold to Portugal and several countries in South America.

During fighting on the island of Crete in 1941, Commonwealth troops fired the modello 34 against the German airborne forces at Maleme airfield. After the Italian surrender in 1943 and the country had joined the Allies, German troops utilised the modello 34 and 35 as the GeBH-254(i) and GeBH-255(i) respectively. The howitzers were sometimes employed as anti-tank weapons, and the modello 34 was the primary weapon of the Semovente da 75/18 self-propelled artillery piece. The anti-tank effectiveness displayed was produced by the 'effetto pronto' high explosive anti-tank (HEAT) ammunition developed for the role.

The Obice M75/18 modello 34 and modello 35 were both versatile field howitzers that served well in the Italian armed forces.

Obice M75/18 Howitzer modello 34	
Country of Origin	Italy
Calibre	75mm
Crew	6
Range	10,549 yards
Rate of Fire	5 rounds per minute
Number manufactured	600

ABOVE LEFT: Obice M75/18 atop a mountain in Vendone, Liguria, Italy. (CREATIVE COMMONS DAVIDE PAPALINI VIA WIKIMEDIA COMMONS)

ABOVE RIGHT: The self-propelled Semovente 75/18 with the 75mm gun mounted in 1943. (CREATIVE COMMONS BUNDESARCHIV BILD VIA WIKIMEDIA COMMONS)

LEFT: This Obice M75/18 modello 34 is on display at Heraklion, Greece. (CREATIVE COMMONS ZUBISOFT VIA WIKIMEDIA COMMONS)

Anti-tank Guns

The debut of the tank on the battlefield in 1915 transformed the character of land warfare. Early attempts to cope with the armoured fighting vehicle included the heroism of individual soldiers approaching closely enough to throw clusters of hand grenades bound together to disable the steel monsters, dig deep trenches to trap them and other inefficient defensive measures.

Available field artillery pieces were sometimes employed, their angles of fire depressed horizontally, but these were not capable of delivering sufficient firepower on most occasions. Purpose-built heavy calibre anti-tank rifles appeared during World War One and the German Army fielded the 37mm TaK 1918 anti-tank gun. Some field guns were supplied with armour-piercing rounds. The famous French 75mm gun was also used in defence against German tanks, its high muzzle velocity an asset in penetration.

However, it was not until the inter-war years that major powers began to develop anti-tank guns – weapons dedicated to the defence against and destruction of enemy armoured fighting vehicles. While the TaK 1918 was probably the world's first such weapon, anti-tank guns with smaller calibres but high muzzle velocity became a focus. In 1928, the German Bundeswehr introduced the 37mm PaK 36, perhaps the first anti-tank gun that was actually intended to destroy enemy armour rather than just render it inoperable.

During World War Two, the anti-tank gun came into its own, with weapons capable of standing up to the relatively lightly armoured tanks of the early war years. But when heavier armour arrived on the battlefield, the inevitable response was the heavier anti-tank gun. Such progression is well indicated by the step-up of the British Army's 2-pounder, 6-pounder and 17-pounder anti-tank guns. The German Army also built its core anti-tank weapons to heavier calibres with the 75mm PaK 41 and 88mm PaK 43. The latter was related to the 88mm flak cannon that was pressed into service by German forces under the command of General Erwin Rommel in France in 1940 and then in the deserts of North Africa. The 88mm proved deadly in the anti-tank role and became a legend.

The Soviet Red Army deployed the ZiS-2 57mm and 76.2mm ZiS-3 guns along with other field artillery types that served in multiple roles. American anti-tank field weapons likewise evolved from 37mm to the license-built French 75, the 3-inch anti-aircraft gun in the anti-tank role, and the 90mm gun that armed later production tank destroyers.

M3 37mm

Effective Early in the Pacific

The American military establishment was something of a latecomer in the inter-war development of the anti-tank gun. By the 1930s, US Army anti-tank formations were regularly armed with the .50-calibre machine gun. However, observations of German forces in action during the Spanish Civil War prompted the US to procure a pair of the German PaK 36 37mm anti-tank gun for study.

Although an understanding of the German weapon contributed to the development of the M3 37mm, there was at least one marked difference in the new US weapon that was designed and put through trials into 1938. The M3 was built with a single-shot vertical sliding wedge block, while the PaK 36 was semiautomatic with a more complex mechanism. This instance aside, the two shared similar split trail carriages along with elevation and firing systems. Officially adopted by the US Army as a lightweight gun that could be manhandled into firing position if necessary, the M3 and carriage M4 entered production in 1940 and became a common element of the US table of organisation and equipment during the early years of World War Two. The weapon weighed 912lb, fired a 1.92-pound shell just over four miles

and was capable of being towed by the Ford GPW and Willie's jeeps. Its barrel was 6ft, 11in long.

Even as the United States entered World War Two, the M3 was becoming outdated in terms of European improvements in armour. It was incapable of penetrating the frontal armour of German tanks that were fielded by 1942 and 1943 in North Africa. In time, it was replaced by the M1 57mm anti-tank gun, patterned after the British 6-pounder gun. Nevertheless, in the Pacific theatre, the M3 remained effective against Japanese armoured fighting vehicles and provided critical infantry fire support during the pivotal battle for the island of Guadalcanal and elsewhere as Japanese tank development was woefully inadequate during the conflict.

The M3 was manufactured in large numbers before production ended in 1943. It was also employed as the main armament of the Stuart light tank, the secondary weapon of the early M3 Lee/Grant medium tank, aboard the M8 Greyhound armoured car and in other self-propelled systems.

LEFT: M3 37mm anti-tank gun being manhandled at Fort Benning, Georgia, in 1942. (LIBRARY OF CONGRESS VIA WIKIMEDIA COMMONS)

LEFT: This M3 37mm anti-tank gun is being hauled by soldiers into position on the island of Kwajalein in the Pacific. (US DEPARTMENT OF DEFENSE VIA WIKIMEDIA COMMONS)

BELOW: M3 37mm anti-tank gun on display at Fort Sam Houston, Texas, with shield that offered some protection for the crew. (PUBLIC DOMAIN PETER RIMAR VIA WIKIMEDIA COMMONS)

M3 Anti-Tank Gun 37mm	
Country of Origin	United States
Calibre	37mm
Crew	6
Range	4.29 miles
Rate of Fire	25 rounds per minute
Number manufactured	18,702

M5 76mm

Adapted to take on Tanks

While the US Army accepted the M3 37mm anti-tank gun into service, there was already a stirring of interest in the development of a heavier weapon in the American arsenal. Among other projects such as the mounting of the French 75 built under license aboard a half-track as a rudimentary tank destroyer, the 76.2mm anti-aircraft gun T9 caught the eye of enterprising designers.

The marriage of the T9 gun and components of the M2 105mm howitzer led to the prototype M5 76mm anti-tank gun, originally the 3-inch Gun T10, in September 1941. Later standardised as the M3 on carriage M1, production of the M5 got underway in December 1942 with slight revisions occurring with the split trail carriage in late 1943, leading to its designation as M6. The M5 weighed 4,872lb, rather heavy for an infantry support anti-tank gun. Its barrel was 11ft, 2in long, and its maximum range was 9.13 miles. In addition to the carriage, the components borrowed from the 105mm M2 included the hydropneumatic recoil system and horizontal sliding block breech. Muzzle velocity was a significant attribute at 2,600ft per second.

When the M5 was ready for deployment, its reception among the infantry establishment was lukewarm due to its excessive weight. The tank destroyer command was reluctant to take it, preferring the self-propelled guns then in development. Ordered to convert some 15 tank destroyer battalions to the towed gun, the TD command placed 36 M5s in three 12-gun companies with M3 half-tracks provided for towing.

Supplied with the new gun, the 805th Tank Destroyer Battalion arrived in Italy in October 1943 and put the M5 to the test in combat. Difficult terrain and rainy weather taxed its utility. At Mortain, France, during the Normandy campaign in 1944, the 823rd Tank Destroyer Battalion destroyed 14 German tanks, but lost 11 men and 11 of its guns. The M5 was also used in direct fire against enemy strongpoints and as secondary field artillery to provide divisional indirect support. However, its role as an anti-tank gun began to wane as combat personnel preferred self-propelled weapons over the heavy towed variety.

The M5 had been removed from frontline service by 1945. In 1953, it was selected as the gun to fire ceremonial salutes to every newly elected US President and still serves in that role today.

M5 Anti-Tank Gun 76mm	
Country of Origin	United States
Calibre	76.2mm (3-inch)
Crew	9
Range	9.13 miles
Rate of Fire	12 rounds per minute
Number manufactured	2,500

PaK 35/36 37mm & PaK 38 50mm

Successful anti-armour Series

LEFT: German soldiers push a PaK 36 37mm anti-tank gun in France. (CREATIVE COMMONS BUNDESARCHIV BILD VIA WIKIMEDIA COMMONS)

LEFT: German soldiers man a 50mm PaK 38 anti-tank gun in Tunisia in 1943. (CREATIVE COMMONS BUNDESARCHIV BILD VIA WIKIMEDIA COMMONS)

BELOW: A German PaK 36 gun crew seeks a target during the First Battle of Kharkov on the Eastern Front, October 1941. (NATIONAL DIGITAL ARCHIVES OF POLAND VIA WIKIMEDIA COMMONS)

The PaK 36 was deployed during World War Two from the September 1939 invasion of Poland, but during the Battle of France it was deemed ineffective against Allied tanks of the day. By 1941, it was quite effective against early lightly armoured Red Army tanks on the Eastern Front; but the prospect of heavier Soviet tanks led to the decision to replace it by late 1941.

That November, numbers of the heavier 50mm PaK 38 began arriving. The new gun was a revision of an initial Rheinmetall response to German Army requirements. The barrel was substantially longer than predecessors at 10ft, and it fired a shell of nearly five pounds to an effective range of 3,000 yards or nearly two miles.

The PaK 38 reached the Eastern Front in the spring of 1941 and was found capable of penetrating the frontal armour of the famed Soviet T-34 medium tank. The introduction of more powerful anti-tank weapons during the course of the war did not mean the end for the PaK 38, which continued as a frontline Wehrmacht gun through 1945.

First seeing action in the Spanish Civil War of the mid-1930s, the 37mm PaK 36 was the standard issue anti-tank gun of the German Wehrmacht into 1942. It was developed by the German arms manufacturer Rheinmetall beginning in 1933 and entered service with the German Army three years later.

The PaK 36 was a derivative of the Rheinmetall 37mm PaK (Panzerabwehr Kanone) L/45, which emerged in the mid-1920s but became rapidly obsolete amid the realisation that horse-drawn artillery might well become obsolete in the years ahead. With the substitution of the original wooden spoked wheels for magnesium alloys with rubber tyres, the new anti-tank gun was designated the PaK 35/36 and entered service with the Wehrmacht in 1934. The PaK 36, interchangeable with the 35/36 label, remained in production for a decade from 1933 to 1943. It was widely copied by other nations in their own pursuit of an adequate anti-tank weapon. The PaK 36 weighed 990lb and was mounted atop a split trail carriage with a spade at the rear for a steadier firing platform. It operated with a horizontal sliding block breech and buffer-recuperator recoil combination operated by spring via compressing oil.

PaK 35/36 37mm & PaK 38 50mm	
Country of Origin	Germany
Crew	5; 5
Calibre	37mm; 50mm
Range	5,997 yards; 3,000 yards
Rate of Fire	13 rounds per minute; 13 rounds per minute
Number manufactured	20,000; 9,566

PaK 40 75mm

Heavier tanks, heavier Guns

ABOVE: A German PaK 40 gun crew in Albania, 1943. (CREATIVE COMMONS BUNDESARCHIV BILD VIA WIKIMEDIA COMMONS)

RIGHT: In this January 1944 photo, a German tank hunter unit fires at Yugoslav partisans in Bosnia. (CREATIVE COMMONS BUNDESARCHIV BILD VIA WIKIMEDIA COMMONS)

to its weight of 3,142lb. It fired to an effective range of 1,969 yards. Its barrel was 11ft, 4in long, and it operated with a semi-automatic horizontal block breech and hydropneumatic recoil atop a split trail carriage. The gun was transportable by Opel Blitz truck, half-track or tractor, its mobility being one of its greatest challenges on the battlefield.

By the end of 1942, more than 1,300 examples were on the front lines, while some had been supplied to Axis forces in other nations. When the Soviet tanks encountered the PaK 40 they were destroyed in great numbers as the weapon became the primary towed anti-tank gun of German forces in North Africa, Italy and western Europe. The PaK 40 was effective against many Allied tanks and only met difficulty in penetrating the armour of late-generation World War Two heavy tanks such as the Soviet IS-2, the US M26 Pershing, and the British Churchill.

A lighter example of the 75mm gun was used in German aircraft and another model of the PaK 40 was developed as a dual-purpose anti-tank and infantry support/field gun. The PaK 40 remained in use for decades with various armies after the end of World War Two.

As the Pak 38 entered service in 1940 as a replacement for the Pak 36, another anti-tank gun of heavier 75mm calibre was in its design phase. The resulting PaK 40 became the workhorse of the Wehrmacht anti-tank units from its introduction to combat in 1942 through the end of World War Two.

Reports received in Germany of new and more heavily armoured Soviet tanks raised an alarm in 1939. The new and formidable T-34 medium and KV-1 and KV-2 heavy tanks eventually began to emerge on the battlefield more rapidly than anticipated during Operation Barbarossa in June 1941. Although the PaK 40 was on the drawing board, its production did not initially seem urgent, but with an abrupt re-focus, the manufacture of the PaK 40 increased in the autumn of 1941.

The PaK 40 was constructed entirely of steel, which contributed

RIGHT: The PaK 40 75mm gun was the backbone of Wehrmacht anti-tank units from 1942. (CREATIVE COMMONS BALCER-COMMOSWIKI VIA WIKIMEDIA COMMONS)

PaK 40 75mm	
Country of Origin	Germany
Calibre	75mm
Crew	6
Range	1,969 yards
Rate of Fire	14 rounds per minute
Number manufactured	23,300

ZiS-2 57mm

From Stalin's Factory

Early in 1940, the designers at Josef Stalin Factory No 92 in Gorky and their leader, VG Grabin, were thinking about the future of the tank on the battlefield and anticipated a war with Nazi Germany at some point. They considered ways to defeat heavier German tanks that were sure to be developed and concluded that whatever calibre it took to do destroy their own KV-1 heavy tank would be sufficient against the Germans as well.

With that decided, the ensuing trials settled on the 57mm anti-tank gun, that would be named the ZiS-2 (ZiS translated as the honorific slogan 'factory named after Stalin'). The ZiS-2 became the primary anti-tank gun of the Red Army during World War Two. It weighed 2,756lb and its barrel measured 13ft long atop a split trail carriage and utilised a hydropneumatic recoil system along with a semiautomatic vertical sliding wedge breech. Development of the ZiS-2 began in the spring of 1940 and it was accepted for production in June 1941.

Fatefully, the Germans launched the invasion of the Soviet Union in the same month. In a controversial move, Generals NN.Voronev, chief marshal of the artillery, and GL Govorov, a senior officer deemed expert in artillery, jointly ordered a halt to production of the ZiS-2 in December, after only

LEFT: The long barrel of the ZiS-2 anti-tank gun is evident in this example at the Museum of Heroic Defence and Liberation of Sevastopol. (CREATIVE COMMONS CMAPM VIA WIKIMEDIA COMMONS)

LEFT: The Zi-S-2 breech was loaded with a highly effective 57mm round. (CREATIVE COMMONS CMAPM VIA WIKIMEDIA COMMONS)

ZiS-2 57mm	
Country of Origin	Soviet Union
Calibre	57mm
Crew	7
Range	5.21 miles
Rate of Fire	10 rounds per minute
Number manufactured	9,645

371 guns had been completed, while the Red Army struggled to blunt the German drive deep into Russia. Their rationale was somewhat surprising: the 57mm weapon with armour piercing rounds possessed such penetrating power that it passed straight through the relatively thin armour of earlier German tanks without exploding. Production lines dedicated to the ZiS-2 were converted to the ZiS-3 field gun 76mm and lighter 45mm weapons became standard anti-tank guns for a short time.

The future of the ZiS-2 was resolved with the introduction of the heavier PzKpfw V Panther and PzKpfw VI Tiger tanks on the Eastern Front by 1943. Production of the ZiS-2 resumed, and the weapon re-entered the Red Army anti-tank units on June 15, 1943. It served through the end of World War Two and was retired in the 1950s with the introduction of the heavier 100mm gun.

LEFT: The extended elevation of the ZiS-2 gun is demonstrated by this museum example in Poland. (CREATIVE COMMONS WISNIA 6522 VIA WIKIMEDIA COMMONS)

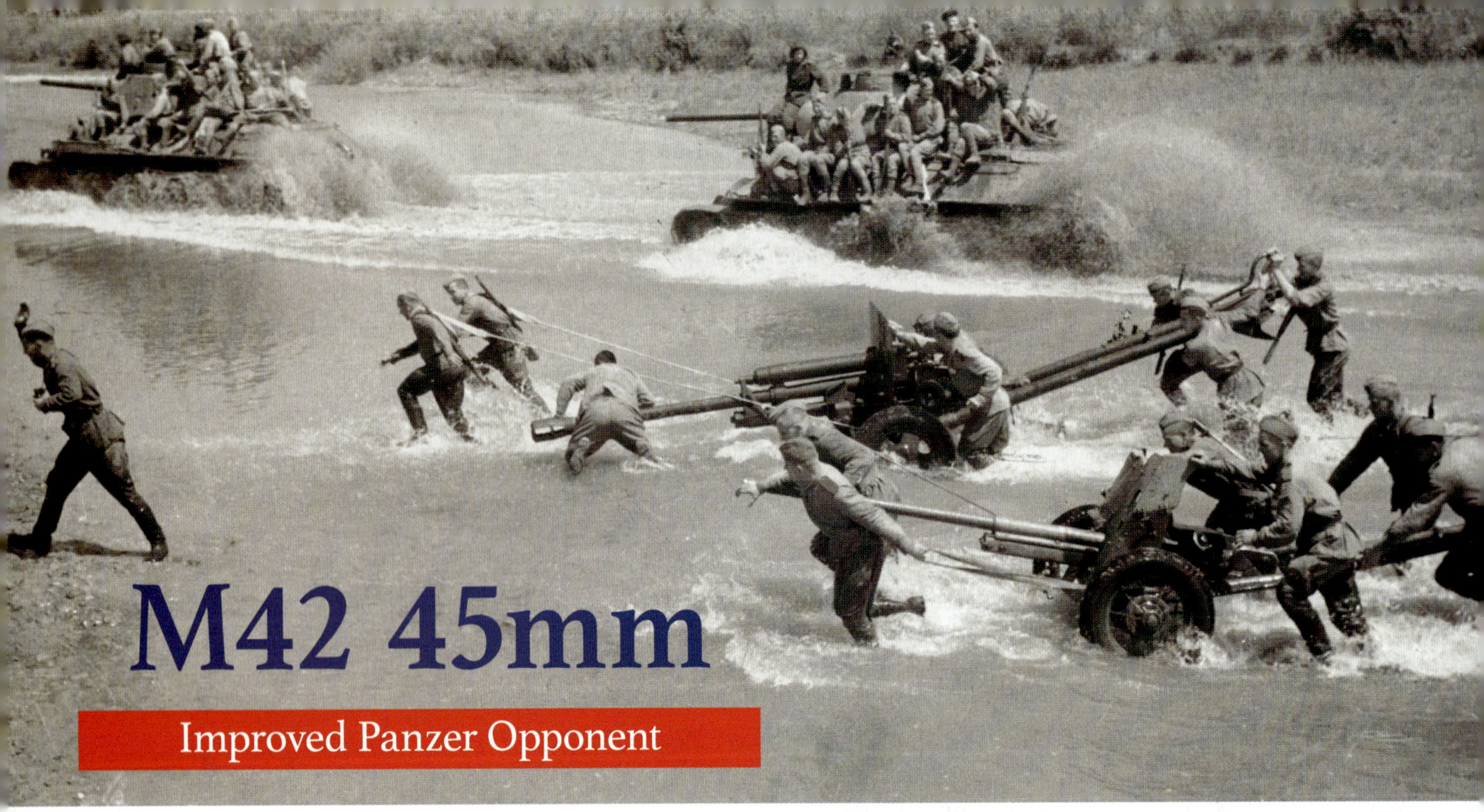

M42 45mm

Improved Panzer Opponent

ABOVE: Soldiers of the 1st Ukrainian Front cross a river in July 1944. The weapon in the foreground is an M42. (TASS RIA NOVOSTI VIA WIKIMEDIA COMMONS)

RIGHT: This M42 45mm anti-tank gun in a street depiction at a Hungarian museum. (CREATIVE COMMONS GNU FREE DOCUMENTATION LICENSE VIA WIKIMEDIA COMMONS)

Soviet arms production facility No 172 at Motovillikha brought the M42 45mmm anti-tank gun from drawing board to production as a replacement for the older M1937 anti-tank gun K-53, with the new gun named for its year of service entry.

Although the M42 shared several characteristics with its predecessor, improvements were made to include a longer barrel at nearly 10ft, more powerful ammunition and a shield for the crew that was more substantial at a thickness of 2.76in. The gun shield was also made with hinges to produce a less substantial silhouette in concealment and to ease transport. When the gun shield was folded in action,

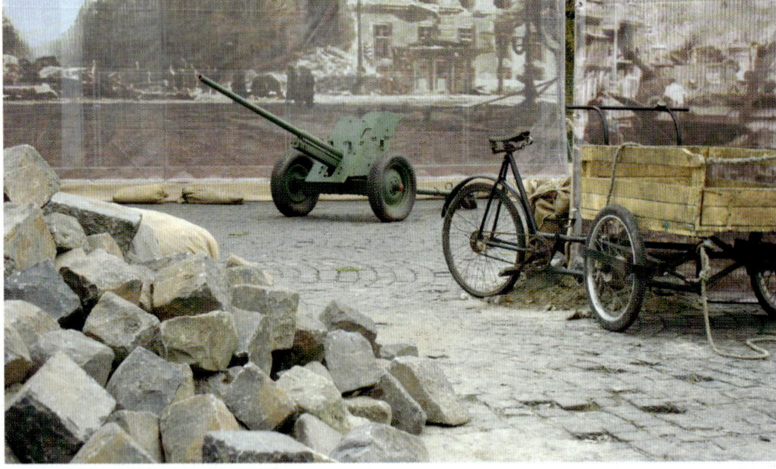

M42 45mm	
Country of Origin	Soviet Union
Calibre	45mm
Crew	6
Range	2.84 miles
Rate of Fire	20 rounds per minute
Number manufactured	10,843

crewmembers were often obliged to work on their bellies or at least crouch to avoid enemy small-arms fire and artillery fragments.

The M1942 weighed 1,378lb and fired with a semi-automatic vertical sliding wedge breech and hydrospring recoil system. Its split trail carriage employed pneumatic tyres for rapid movement cross-country or over the road. The gun made its debut in combat during 1942 and for a while became the primary weapon of its kind against early German panzers, its shell more effective in killing the enemy tanks than the larger contemporary ZiS-2 57mm gun. However, the arrival of the medium PzKpfw V Panther and heavy PzKpfw VI Tiger tanks in German divisions compelled the Soviets to renew the production of the ZiS-2 in late 1942 as the 45mm shell was inadequate to stop the heavier German armour.

Nevertheless, the M1942 remained in service with the Red Army throughout World War Two, its high rate of fire in the anti-tank role with armour piercing rounds or against enemy infantry concentrations with fragmentation shells providing welcome support in the field. The M42 was relatively cheap to produce and its versatility added to its longevity. Reports have been received that elderly examples of the M42 were pressed into service by Russian troops in Ukraine in 2025.

RIGHT: With the gun shield open, this M42 45mm anti-tank gun is idle as its crew rests in 1945. (CREATIVE COMMONS HANS SOOSAAR VIA WIKIMEDIA COMMONS)

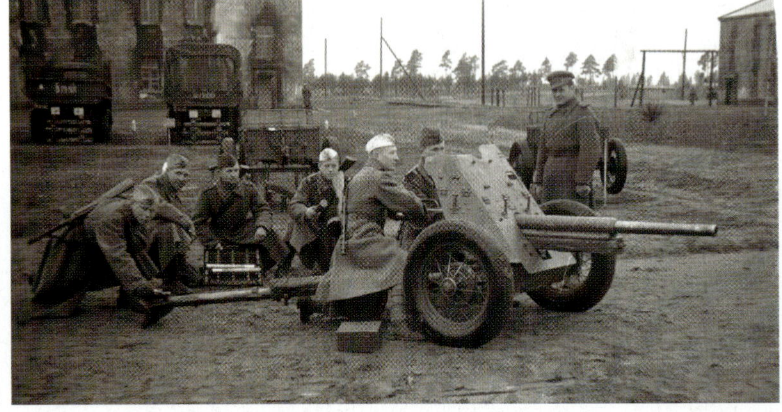

Type 1 AT Gun 47mm

Rapid Fire in the Pacific

Intended to replace the earlier Type 94 37mm anti-tank gun against enemy armour across the Pacific and on the Asian continent during World War Two, the Type 1 AT Gun 47mm made its combat debut in 1941. The full name of the Japanese weapon was the Type 1 Mobile 47mm Rapid-Firing Gun, and it lived up to its moniker.

The Type 1 was developed in 1939 and was named for its introduction year of '2601' according to the Japanese calendar. The real impetus for the emergence of the Type 1 was the experience against Soviet tanks in the border clashes of 1939 as heavier Red Army armoured fighting vehicles were expected in the future and the Type 94 was believed inadequate to neutralise them.

The new Type 1 weighed 1,660lb and was configured for transport by motorised vehicle. Its barrel was 8ft, 4in long, and the gun fired a shell that was just over three pounds to a maximum range of nearly 7,500 yards. The weapon operated with a semiautomatic horizontal sliding breech block and

Type 1 At Gun 47mm	
Country of Origin	Japan
Calibre	47mm
Crew	3
Range	7,546 yards
Rate of Fire	15 rounds per minute
Number manufactured	2,300

hydrospring recoil system with split trail carriage.

In action, the Type 1 earned the grudging respect of its US adversaries, who called it an "excellent weapon with mechanised carriage and a high muzzle velocity." With that velocity, the Type 1 was capable of penetrating the armour of the M4 Sherman medium tank at 800 yards. It was widely used in the Pacific against armour and as a beach defence gun against landing craft. It was notable in that role at Peleliu, as well as across the Philippines and through the 82 days of the fight for Okinawa. The gun was also mounted as the main armament of the Type 1 Chi Ha medium tank.

The Type 1 was consistently effective against Allied light tanks such as the M3 Stuart but was deemed inferior to contemporary anti-tank guns of other countries. As M4 medium tanks were improved, its rounds had less success against frontal armour and often targeted the flanks and exposed undersides of the vehicles.

ABOVE: This Type 1 47mm anti-tank gun was captured on the island of Guam in 1944. (US DEPARTMENT OF DEFENSE VIA WIKIMEDIA COMMONS)

LEFT: Knocked out M4 Sherman tanks are visible in the distance from this Type 1 position at Okinawa. (GOVERNMENT OF JAPAN VIA WIKIMEDIA COMMONS)

LEFT: Type 1 47mm anti-tank gun on display at the US Army Museum in Honolulu, Hawaii. (PUBLIC DOMAIN MAX SMITH VIA WIKIMEDIA COMMONS)

Modele 1937 APX 47mm

A Successor to the 75

ABOVE: This Modele 1937 APX 47mm anti-tank gun is displayd at the Base Borden Museum in Ontario, Canada. (CREATIVE COMMONS BALCER VIA WIKIMEDIA COMMONS)

RIGHT: The semiautomatic breech of the APX 47mm. (CREATIVE COMMONS BALCER VIA WIKIMEDIA COMMONS)

RIGHT: French gunners operating an AC 47mm on the Maginot Line. (ASSOCIATION DES AMIS DE LA LIGNE MAGINOT VIA WIKIMEDIA COMMONS)

Modele 1937 APX 47mm	
Country of Origin	France
Calibre	47mm
Crew	6
Range	2,187 yards
Rate of Fire	15 rounds per minute
Number manufactured	1,268

By the 1930s, the French military establishment had come to the realisation that its venerable Model 1897 75mm gun might be trending toward inferior performance amid the growing division of labour among artillery pieces. To that end, the development of a purpose built anti-tank gun was undertaken by 1936. The result was the APX 47mm anti-tank gun, smaller and lighter than the older Model 1897.

The APX name was an abbreviation for the designer, the state-run Atelier de Construction de Puteaux, and the new gun provided satisfactory results against the thin armour of early German tanks. With an armour piercing shell that weighed about 3.75lb, the gun could penetrate approximately 2.4in of armour at a distance of 600 yards. The APX 47mm gun weighed 2,359lb and was carried atop a split trail carriage. Its barrel was 8ft, 2in long, and the gun operated with a semi-automatic horizontal sliding wedge breech block and hydrospring recoil system. It was built for transport by motor vehicle and a close variant, the Modele 1939, was also briefly in production.

When World War Two broke out in 1939 and France fell in the spring of 1940, the Modele 1937 and 1939 APX had been fielded in only small numbers. The Germans captured most of them, renamed them the 47mm PaK 181(f) and 183(f) respectively and used them as main weapons with some self-propelled tank destroyers or as coastal defence along the Atlantic Wall.

Another similar anti-tank gun, the AC 47mm, was developed in the 1930s for use with the fixed fortifications of the Maginot Line. The AC 47 was described as 'anti char' for its anti-tank role and was found in the casemates and turrets of the post-war French defensive front. Due to its primary function, tit was constructed with little mobility and was intentionally built so that it could not turn and potentially fire against friendly troops if captured.

Ordnance QF 2-pounder & 6-pounder

Early anti-armour Entries

The Ordnance QF (quick firing) 2-pounder and 6-pounder guns were mainstays of the British Army anti-tank field units during World War Two, especially during the early years. The 2-pounder (40mm) was developed as a tank-mounted anti-tank weapon manufactured by Vickers-Armstrong and accepted for service in October 1935, while the 6-pounder (57mm) was designed by the Woolwich Arsenal after a gun widely used in the Royal Navy in the 19th Century. The 6-pounder was delayed in production until November 1941 entering service with the army the following spring. Production of both guns ended in 1945.

The 2-pounder weighed 1,795lb and operated on three-leg platform carriages from both Vickers-Armstrong and Woolwich Arsenal. Its barrel was 6ft, 10in long, and it fired via a semiautomatic vertical sliding block breech and hydrospring recoil system. It was the primary anti-tank weapon fielded with the British Expeditionary Force that deployed to France in the opening months of World War Two. Many of them were lost prior to the evacuation from Dunkirk in 1940.

Though outclassed by improved German tank armour by 1942, the 2-pounder continued in the anti-tank role in the North Africa campaign. Despite its later obsolescence as an anti-tank gun, it remained in service throughout the war and was deployed subsequently with Home Guard units as well as with British forces in the

LEFT: Ordnance QF 6-pounder of the 86th Anti-Tank Regiment during exercises in September 1942. (COLLECTIONS OF THE IMPERIAL WAR MUSEUMS VIA WIKIMEDIA COMMONS)

Pacific and the China-Burma-India theatre, where it remained effective against inferior Japanese tanks throughout.

The 6-pounder began replacing the 2-pounder gradually in 1942 and provided a marked improvement. It was also used by the US Army, built under license as the 57mm Gun M1. The 6-pounder was mounted on a two-leg split trail carriage. It weighed 2,520lb, and its barrel stretched 8ft, 4in. The gun was also operated by the vertical sliding block breech, but featured hydropneumatic recoil. During the course of the war, modifications were made to the weapon, including the lengthening of the barrel in the Mk IV variant and the addition of a muzzle brake.

The 6-pounder was used against Axis forces for the first time at the Battle of Gazala in May 1942 and was credited with disabling the first heavy

Tiger tanks encountered during the desert war. Performing admirably in the desert, it continued in service and was also credited as the first anti-tank gun to destroy a medium Panther tank in Italy. By 1943, the 17-pounder gun (76.2mm) was becoming available and joined the 6-pounder in the field.

During the course of the war, the modified 6-pounder also replaced the main guns of some Churchill, Crusader and other tanks.

Ordnance QF 2-Pounder & 6-Pounder	
Country of Origin	Great Britain
Calibre	40mm; 57mm
Crew	5; 6
Range	1,800 yards; 1,650 yards
Number manufactured	12,000; 20,000+

BELOW LEFT: An Ordnance 2-pounder gun crew prepares to fire in September 1942. (COLLECTIONS OF THE IMPERIAL WAR MUSEUMS VIA WIKIMEDIA COMMONS)

BELOW RIGHT: Canadian soldiers fire a 6-pounder anti-tank gun in 1943. (COLLECTIONS OF THE IMPERIAL WAR MUSEUMS VIA WIKIMEDIA COMMONS)

Ordnance QF 17-pounder

Urgent anti-tank Answer

As armour protection increased with new designs of tanks and armoured fighting vehicles through World War Two, so too the calibre and muzzle velocity of anti-tank guns increased. Evidence of this progression is seen within the development of the Ordnance QF 17-pounder.

Recognising the urgency of the situation, the British military establishment sought a heavier weapon than the existing 2-pounder and 6-pounder guns then available or in development. The effort began in 1940, with the design of the 17-pounder (76.2mm) gun completed by late 1941, a prototype was built and initial production began within a few months. Vickers Armstrong got the programme underway and, shortly after, reports of a new and quite threatening German tank type, the PzKpfw VI Tiger, in North Africa raised new alarms.

In response, the first 100 production 17-pounder guns were shipped to North Africa atop carriages originally intended for the QF 25-pounder howitzer. Nicknamed 'Pheasant', this prototype gun was deployed into desert action in February 1943. At the same time, work on the full production 17-pounder proceeded and production began within weeks.

The 17-pounder gun weighed 2,032lb and had a vertical sliding breech block, hydropneumatic recoil and split trail carriage with substantial gun shield. Its barrel stretched 13ft, 9in, and it paired a muzzle velocity of 2,900ft per second with an armour piercing discarding sabot round that was effective against contemporary German tanks. Some military

observers deemed the 17-pounder the finest weapon of its kind to enter service with Allied forces during World War Two.

The gun was built in more than half-a-dozen variants or marks during the war years and was adapted as the main armament for tanks and self-propelled assault vehicles. These included the M10 tank destroyer, to produce the Achilles and Valentine tank chassis in the Archer. The most famous combination was with the turret of the US-built M4 Sherman medium tank. Nicknamed the 'Firefly', this combination saw wide deployment during the final months of the war.

The 17-pounder remained in common use through the Korean War and is still in service with some countries today.

Ordnance QF 17-Pounder	
Country of Origin	Great Britain
Calibre	76.2mm
Crew	6
Range	6.5 miles
Rate of Fire	10 rounds per minute
Number manufactured	2,700

Hotchkiss 25mm

French anti-armour Awakening

in May 1940, many were believed to be in service. When the British Expeditionary Force arrived in France, a number of the Hotchkiss 25mms were issued to them as well. A few examples had seen action during the Spanish Civil War of the mid-1930s and the gun underwent modifications through 1937.

The Hotchkiss 25mm weighed 1,060lb. It operated with a semiautomatic vertical breech block, hydraulic buffer and spring recoil system and split trail carriage that provided for wide traverse, utilising spades to stabilise the firing platform and allowing the gun to be fired while its wheels were still engaged. The barrel was 5ft, 11in long and fired a shell of just under a pound on a maximum range of 1.1 miles.

In combat, the 25mm proved capable of penetrating the armour of early German tanks, but was usually incapable of completely destroying them or inflicting substantial casualties on their crews. Large numbers of the guns were captured during the Battle of France, with the Germans redeploying them as the 25mm PaK 112(f) or 113(f).

LEFT: A German soldier marches French prisoners past a captured Hotchkiss 25m gun in 1940. (PUBLIC DOMAIN ERIC BORCHERT VIA WIKIMEDIA COMMONS)

LEFT: British soldiers load a Hotchkiss 25mm anti-tank gun in November 1939. (COLLECTIONS OF THE IMPERIAL WAR MUSEUMS VIA WIKIMEDIA COMMONS)

Hotchkiss 25mm	
Country of Origin	France
Calibre	25mm
Crew	4
Range	1.1 miles
Rate of Fire	15 rounds per minute
Number manufactured	6,000

Perhaps ahead of other military forces around the world, the French Army was well aware by the mid-1920s that their existing weapons might become obsolete on the battlefield as tanks and armoured fighting vehicles exhibited heavier weapons and greater protection against enemy fire. In fact, the French had experimented with armour piercing ammunition during World War One.

The existing French 37mm TRP infantry gun was perceived as inadequate and, in 1926, the historic firm of Hotchkiss et Cie responded to the call for a new anti-tank gun with its Canon de 25mm Semiautomatique Modele 1934.

Nine years after its design was completed, the French Army adopted the Hotchkiss 25mm anti-tank gun, which was expected to provide a solid punch, along with ease of mobility with infantry units on the battlefield. On the eve of World War Two, the Hotchkiss was the primary gun of its type with French forces. When the Germans invaded France and the Low Countries

LEFT: This Hotchkiss 25mm anti-tank gun resides in the Saumur Museum in the Loire Valley in France. (CREATIVE COMMONS PPPACHY VIA WIKIMEDIA COMMONS)

Cannone da 90/53

Dual role for Il Duce

ABOVE: This Cannone da 90/53 is shown on its four-wheel carriage at the Museum of the Battle of El Alamein. (CREATIVE COMMONS COTTON VIA WIKIMEDIA COMMONS)

Cannone da 90/53	
Country of Origin	Italy
Calibre	90mm
Crew	6
Range	19,030 yards horizontal
Rate of Fire	19 rounds per minute
Number manufactured	539

Despite its effectiveness, Ansaldo and the rest of the Italian industrial base were never able to manufacture and deliver the Cannone da 90/53 in the numbers requested by the Italian military. An original order for 1,804 was placed, but only 539 had been completed by the time of the Italian armistice in 1943. When German forces captured examples of the weapon, they were placed in service with the Wehrmacht as the 90mm Flak 309/I(i).

After World War Two, the gun remained in service with other countries, and its use during the Croatian war of independence during the 1990s has been documented.

The Ansaldo company undertook the design of a heavy anti-aircraft gun for the Italian Navy in the mid-1930s and had developed the weapon sufficiently by 1938. At the same time, a land variant of the gun intended for the dual role of antiaircraft and anti-tank performance was introduced. The Cannone da 90/53 indicated that the bore of the gun was 90mm with a barrel of 53 calibre lengths or 4ft, 5in.

The new land weapon entered production in 1939 and had three variants: one that was vehicle towed, another for static emplacement and the third for mounting aboard heavy trucks or other vehicles. The Cannone da 90/53 weighed 19,730lb and utilised a horizontal sliding breech block with recoil cylinders operated via compressed fluid. It fired a 22.71-pound shell to an altitude of 12,000ft in the anti-aircraft role and with a maximum horizontal range of 19,030 yards.

In action, the Cannone da 90/53 proved one of the most effective anti-aircraft guns of World War Two, and when employed against enemy tanks it performed on a level comparable to that of the German 88mm flak gun. At times, it was used to provide indirect fire in infantry support as well. Some sources attest that the gun made its combat debut at the Battle of Arras during the 1940 campaign in France, but it came into wider use during the fighting in North Africa.

RIGHT: This Cannone da 90/53 is shown mounted in the bed of a Lancia truck in February 1943. (GOVERNMENT OF AUSTRALIA VIA WIKIMEDIA COMMONS)

RIGHT: This Cannone da 90/53 is shown still emplaced in coastal defence. (CREATIVE COMMONS ARTIGIANO58 VIA WIKIMEDIA COMMONS)

Anti-aircraft Guns

Defence of Airspace

With the ascendancy of air power in warfare during the first half of the 20th Century, methods of restricting their influence on the battlefield and assertion of control of the air were devised and then steadily improved to counter the performance of modern warplanes.

While the earliest form of anti-aircraft gun was utilised in the Franco-Prussian War to counter the use of observation balloons, World War One required advances in defensive weaponry. This took the form of machine guns adapted for use against low-flying aircraft, balloons floated above key positions, their cables intended to deter encroachment or snare hostile planes and cause them to crash and the adaptation of field artillery pieces available at the time to air defence.

By the inter-war years, field guns and newly developed anti-aircraft guns were being tested and manufactured for specialised mounts that allowed elevations sufficient to fire at high angles. Rapid-fire mechanisms that produced a volume of fire against attacking planes, the introduction of improved target acquisition and ranging equipment to later include radar tracking and sighting and the use of early analogue computers to assist in the process brought anti-aircraft guns to the cutting edge of technology. The analogue computers, for example, were capable of calculating both aiming and firing to improve accuracy and were often implemented with centralised control over a number of widespread gun emplacements.

One of the greatest improvements in anti-aircraft gun lethality during World War Two lay in the development of the proximity fuse. This was effective because it did not require a direct hit against the target. Set to detonate at a specific altitude and with the use of radio equipment, its explosive impact need only be near enough to the enemy aircraft to inflict sufficient damage to bring the plane down.

Among the most effective anti-aircraft guns of World War Two

were weapons made by neutral countries: the 40mm Bofors from Sweden and the 20mm Oerlikon from Switzerland. The Bofors gun was developed in the 1930s and saw wide use during World War Two among both Allied and Axis forces. The Oerlikon was developed by the late 1930s from an earlier German design and was also frequently used by both Axis and Allied forces. Other effective anti-aircraft guns of World War Two included the famed German 88mm flak gun, the US 90mm gun and .50-calibre machine gun in appropriate configuration, the British QF 3.7-inch gun and the Japanese Type 96 25mm.

TOP: A British Auxiliary Territorial spotter uses binoculars beside a **QF 3.7-in anti-aircraft gun in 1942.** (COLLECTIONS OF THE IMPERIAL WAR MUSEUMS VIA WIKIMEDIA COMMONS)

ABOVE: The American **M45 Quad mount supported four .50-calibre anti-aircraft machine guns.** (CREATIVE COMMONS B25ES VIA WIKIMEDIA COMMONS)

LEFT: German troops used this **Model 1909 Krupp field gun in an anti-aircraft role during World War One.** (WORLD TODAY MAGAZINE US GOVERNMENT VIA WIKIMEDIA COMMONS)

M1 Dual Purpose 90mm

American Air Defence Standard

O n June 9, 1938, the US Army issued requirements for a new 90mm anti-aircraft gun that would replace older 76.2mm M1918 and M3 weapons. At the same time, a larger 120mm gun was also specified.

In response, the M1 90mm gun was produced with increased elevation but still sufficient for crewmen to raise a single round and load through the breech of the weapon as it was trained skyward. The T1 mount was developed concurrently, and testing was positive to the extent that a contemporary mount for the 76.2mm guns was cancelled just as it was slated to enter production. Progressive work on the 90mm gun led to the approval of a second prototype on March 21, 1940, and this type entered production later that year. Steady improvements led to the designation of the M1A1, M2 and M3 guns and Allis-Chalmers delivered the first 300 mounts beginning in September 1941.

The M1 90mm was usually deployed in groups of four in the primary role. These were controlled by Kerrison fire predictors or M7 or M9 primitive gun directors. The gun fired armour piercing or high explosive shells weighing approximately 24-pounds to a maximum altitude of more than 43,000ft. It weighed approximately 19,000lb and its barrel stretched nearly 16ft, 7in. It was regularly towed to firing position by the M4 high speed tractor and could be fired while still mounted on its wheels, improving time from transport to engaging the enemy.

The M1 90mm became the standard US anti-aircraft gun of World War Two, while the 120mm M1 was also deployed. The 90mm was continually upgraded during the conflict, with the addition of a searchlight for nocturnal use, the introduction of SCR-584

microwave radar in 1944 and the Bell Labs M3 gun data computer.

Like its British and German heavy counterparts, the M1 90mm was also used in an anti-tank role, although its barrel lacked sufficient depression capability to be thoroughly efficient. The gun was the main armament of the heavy M26 Pershing tank that appeared late in World War Two and the M36 Jackson tank destroyer. It remained in service into the 1950s.

M1 Dual Purpose 90mm	
Country of Origin	United States
Calibre	90mm
Crew	8
Range	43,500 feet altitude
Rate of Fire	10 rounds per minute
Number manufactured	133,833

M1 37mm Gun

Mobile, Light Air Defence Weapon

The primary gun issued to mobile light anti-aircraft units of the US Army on the eve of World War Two, the M1 37mm originated in the mid-1930s as an air defence autocannon. Each battalion of the army's Anti-aircraft Artillery Auto-Weapons organisation was issued a total of 32 of these guns in four batteries of eight.

The M1 37mm had been designed by Browning and was typically towed by a jeep or other vehicles or mounted alongside a pair of Browning M2 heavy .50-calibre machine guns in the bed of the M2 half-track. These combinations were designated the M15 and M15A1 multiple gun motor carriages. The weapon weighed 6,130lb and fired a 1.5-pound shell to an altitude of 27,000ft with a muzzle velocity of 2,598ft per second, and its barrel was just over 6ft,6in long. It fired via a vertical sliding block breech with hydrospring recoil and was typically mounted on the M3/M4 split trail carriage. The M1 37mm gun was sometimes joined with the M1 remote control system and M5 power generation unit in the field and was intended to function in the anti-tank role as well. A modified version was mounted in the Stuart light tank series.

The 37mm gun was versatile, but ineffective against higher altitude aircraft. It was deployed aboard naval patrol boats and in coastal defence emplacements, but as World War Two continued, it was replaced largely by the Swedish 40mm Bofors gun. The M1 37mm was deployed in the Pacific at the outbreak of the war and was used by US and Filipino soldiers in the Philippines during the fighting on the Bataan peninsula and the island of Corregidor. At Guadalcanal, the towed 37mm gun was used in an anti-personnel role with devastating effect against Japanese troop concentrations during the pivotal Battle of the Tenaru (actually the Ilu) River in August 1942.

Although the gun was unable to penetrate the armour of improved contemporary German tanks in the European theatre, it remained effective against Japanese armoured vehicles throughout the Pacific War. Production ended in 1943 as the Bofors became more readily available.

M1 37mm Gun	
Country of Origin	United States
Calibre	37mm
Crew	7
Range	18,897 feet altitude
Rate of Fire	90 rounds per minute
Number manufactured	7,278

ABOVE: This 37mm anti-aircraft gun in a defensive position at an airfield. (US AIR FORCE HISTORICAL RESEARCH AGENCY VIA WIKIMEDIA COMMONS)

LEFT: M1 37mm antiaircraft gun is shown in a log-reinforced emplacement in the Solomon Islands. (PUBLIC DOMAIN W WOLNY VIA WIKIMEDIA COMMONS)

LEFT: This 37mm anti-aircraft gun is mounted aboard a naval patrol boat in the Dutch East Indies. (NATIONAL ARCHIVES OF THE NETHERLANDS VIA WIKIMEDIA COMMONS)

Flak 18 88mm

Iconic Series in Wehrmacht Service

Perhaps the most famous and feared artillery piece of World War Two, the German Flak 18 88mm and its improved variants, the Flak 36, 37 and 41, were versatile on the battlefield in the anti-aircraft role, and also as anti-tank and direct or indirect infantry support weapons.

The inter-war years did not deter Germany from developing a new generation of weapons as the terms of the Treaty of Versailles were ignored, first in secret and then quite openly by the mid-1930s. The German arms manufacturer Krupp owned a majority interest in the Swedish Bofors firm, and the research that produced the 88mm Flak 18 was undertaken there after an early 75mm weapon was considered too small in calibre. The first prototype 88 was built in 1928.

The original Flak 18 was placed atop a cross-shaped gun carriage which allowed the weapon to be fired while its wheels were still engaged. In the field, the gun was highly mobile, but its significant weight of 16,330lb restricted its towing to the largest of vehicles, such as the half-track Sd.Kfz 7. The Flak 18 barrel was just over 16ft, 2in long. The gun exhibited excellent elevation from -3° to 85°, the former a great asset in the anti-tank role. It operated with a semiautomatic horizontal sliding block breech and hydropneumatic recoil. Later variants were fielded with the Flak 36, featuring an improved carriage and two-piece barrel, while the Flak 37 improved fire control and the Flak 41 had a second increase in barrel length.

Mass production of the Flak 18 began in 1933 and it was the centrepiece of Luftwaffe anti-aircraft defence throughout World War Two. The weapons were deployed with analogue computer gunnery assistance and early radar such as the famous Wurzburg series. However, it was in the anti-tank role that the Flak 18 gained lasting fame and it was used in the Spanish Civil War of the mid-1930s. Its ability to penetrate the thick armour of British Matilda II and French Char B1 bis tanks was dramatically demonstrated during the Battle of France, when the 88s were depressed to horizontal firing position on orders from General Erwin Rommel, then commanding the 7th Panzer Division, at Arras in the spring of 1940.

The 88mm Flak 18 and its improved variants served in North Africa, Italy and on the Eastern Front. In western Europe, the weapon was deadly against Allied armour during the fighting toward the German frontier. For Allied troops, it was a scourge and many of them considered every enemy artillery piece encountered to be a dreaded '88'.

Flak 18 88mm	
Country of Origin	Germany
Calibre	88mm
Crew	10
Range	26,000 feet altitude; 16,250 yards ground
Rate of Fire	15 rounds per minute
Number manufactured	21,310

Flak 38 105mm & Flak 40 128mm

High Altitude in Reich Defence

The Flak 38 105mm and Flak 40 128mm guns were heavier complements to the ubiquitous Flak 18 88mm family that defined German anti-aircraft weapons during World War Two. Both were designed and manufactured by Rheinmetall; the Flak 38 in 1933 and the Flak 40 three years later.

The Flak 38 was intended to bring down high-flying enemy aircraft that were technically beyond the range of the Flak 18. Its maximum altitude reached to more than 37,000ft. The gun was constructed in both land and naval variants, the latter forming the anti-aircraft defences of Nazi Kriegsmarine warships such as *Bismarck* and *Tirpitz* and the battlecruisers *Scharnhorst* and *Gneisenau* among others. The land type was essentially an upsized version of the Flak 18 with identical elevation characteristics, breech and recoil systems. Its tremendous weight of 22,540 lb restricted its use in the field and relegated it to fixed coastal and city defences in many cases. An improved version, the Flak 39, substituted an original electrical aiming system with a mechanical apparatus. The barrel length was 18ft, 2in and the gun fired a hefty 33-pound shell.

ABOVE: Crewmen operate a 105mm Flak 38 anti-aircraft gun in coastal defence. (CREATIVE COMMONS BUNDESARCHIV BILD VIA WIKIMEDIA COMMONS)

LEFT: A 128mm Flak 40 heavy anti-aircraft gun in a static mounting. (US GOVERNMENT VIA WIKIMEDIA COMMONS)

The 128mm Flak 40 has been assessed as quite effective in its anti-aircraft role, with the first prototype delivered for evaluation in 1937 and production beginning in 1942. However, the gun weighed more than 37,000lb, requiring transportation in two components. Issues with the firing platform eventually resolved that the gun would be anchored into concrete with heavy bolts. The gun was mounted atop rail cars for improved mobility, but its major contribution to German air defence came with the massive flak towers that protected cities during the Allied bombing campaign from 1943 through the end of the war. These were often placed in twin mounts and operated in Berlin, Hamburg and Vienna most notably. The gun's barrel was 25ft, 7in long and it fired a 57-pound shell to an altitude of more than 48,000ft using a horizontal sliding block breech and hydropneumatic recoil.

LEFT: Captured during World War Two, this 105mm Flak 38 is now in a museum in Moscow. (CREATIVE COMMONS DON-VIP VIA WIKIMEDIA COMMONS)

Flak 38 105mm & Flak 40 128mm	
Country of Origin	Germany
Calibre	105mm; 128mm
Crew	10; 5
Range	37,400 feet; 48,000 feet altitude
Rate of Fire	15 rounds per minute; 10 rounds per minute
Number manufactured	4,200; 1,125

Bofors 40mm & Oerlikon 20mm

ABOVE LEFT: A single-mount 40mm Bofors on outdoor display at a Canadian museum. (CREATIVE COMMONS BALCER-CONNONSWIKI VIA WIKIMEDIA COMMONS)

ABOVE RIGHT: British crewmen train their Bofors 40mm anti-aircraft gun skyward. (US NATIONAL ARCHIVES AND RECORDS ADMINISTRATION VIA WIKIMEDIA COMMONS)

Developed and manufactured in Sweden and Switzerland respectively, these two guns produced by neutral countries were widely used by both Axis and Allied forces during World War Two.

An anti-aircraft autocannon, the Bofors 40mm gun was intended for intermediate use, more powerful than the light machine guns and smaller weapons available in the inter-war years, while never intended to take on high-flying aircraft. The weapon originated with the Swedish Navy's request for a replacement weapon for the Vickers 2-pounder in the 1920s. Subsequently, the German manufacturer Krupp purchased an interest in Bofors. The gun was designed for the export market, selling rapidly by 1932, and on the eve of World War Two in Europe was in service with at least 18 countries. It was built under license across Europe and adopted by the US military in the spring of 1941.

The Bofors 40mm gun weighed 4,367lb and was mounted on a towed four-wheel carriage for ease of movement in battlefield deployment. The gun was also developed in a naval variant that saw wide use. Its barrel was7ft, 5in long, and it could fire a two-pound shell to an altitude of more than 23,000ft.

The Swiss Oerlikon 20mm actually originated with a German design by engineer Reinhold Becker in the 1920s. The Becker design was transferred to the Swiss company SEMAG due to restrictions in production imposed by the Treaty of Versailles after World War One. The resulting weapon derived took its name from the Oerlikon company that acquired SEMAG when that business failed financially.

The Oerlikon 20mm design was completed by 1935 and the weapon entered production two years later. It was widely built under license throughout World War Two and appeared in all theatres of operations both as an anti-aircraft weapon and a naval cannon fed by ammunition drums with multiple rounds. While the 20mm Oerlikon was light – in full mount its weight commonly exceeded 1,000lb – its barrel was slightly longer than 4ft, 5in. The US Navy adopted the 20mm Oerlikon to replace the .50-calibre machine gun in the autumn of 1940.

Bofors 40mm & Oerlikon 20mm	
Country of Origin	Sweden; Switzerland
Calibre	40mm; 20mm
Crew	4; 4
Range	23,490; 22,200 feet altitude
Rate of Fire	140 rounds per minute; 320 rounds per minute
Number manufactured	60,000+; 124,000+

RIGHT: A row of 20mm Oerlikon anti-aircraft guns aboard the aircraft carrier USS *Hornet* in 1945. (US NAVY VIA WIKIMEDIA COMMONS)

72-K 25mm

The 72-K entered production in 1941 and other manufacturing facilities joined the effort to deliver 300 weapons to the Red Army in the first year. Approximately 200 of the guns were eventually mounted on the bed of the GAZ-MM light truck and more were placed on the ZiS-11. Others were mounted on rail cars or in static positions for air defence.

The 72-K was widely distributed within the Red Army. With a muzzle velocity of 3,000ft per second, its 25mm round was capable of penetrating the armour of light tanks and other vehicles, while the gun could be depressed to an elevation of -10° for use against land targets, including enemy infantry.

The 72-K remained in service after World War Two and was widely exported to Soviet client states. It was withdrawn from Red Army service in 1960 in favour of the Zu 23-2 23mm gun. Between 600 and 700 were lost in action during the Great Patriotic War.

LEFT: The GAZ-MM light truck was often used as a firing platform. (CREATIVE COMMONS ANDSHEL VIA WIKIMEDIA COMMONS)

Under chief designer Mikhail Loginov and the immediate supervision of Lev Loktev, the 72-K 25mm anti-aircraft gun was developed at the 8th Kalinin Artillery Plant beginning in 1939 as a follow-on to the larger 37mm automatic air defence gun M1939. In combat, it proved highly effective from a manually operated perspective, firing with seven-round clips against low flying aircraft.

Topping a four-wheel carriage with two stabilising outriggers, the K-72 was protected by a gun shield installed in production models from 1943, and was aimed manually without the use of centralised or external fire control. It weighed 2,670lb, with the ammunition clips fed from above into a feeding tray to facilitate the automatic firing mechanism. Its barrel was nearly 6¼ft long and the gun was capable of an elevation of 85°. The high rate of fire at 240 rounds per minute often caused the weapon's single barrel to overheat. An automated sight was introduced in 1943, and the gun was highly mobile being towed by light trucks at a maximum road speed of just over 37mph.

LEFT: This 72-K 25mm anti-aircraft gun with gun shield resides in St Petersburg, Russia. (CREATIVE COMMONS САЙГА20K VIA WIKIMEDIA COMMONS)

72-K 25mm	
Country of Origin	Soviet Union
Calibre	25mm
Crew	6
Range	7,900 feet altitude
Rate of Fire	240 rounds per minute
Number manufactured	4,860

LEFT: Shown at combat elevation, this 72-K anti-aircraft gun is situated atop the standard wheeled carriage. (CREATIVE COMMONS САЙГА20K VIA WIKIMEDIA COMMONS)

61-K 37mm

Soviet Adaptation Of Swedish Bofors

RIGHT: Red Army crew and their 61-K 37mm anti-aircraft gun in Crimea, 1944. (GOVERNMENT OF THE RUSSIAN FEDERATION VIA WIKIMEDIA COMMONS)

RIGHT: This 61-K 37mm was used in Indochina against the French in the 1950s after surviving World War Two. (CREATIVE COMMONS BINH GIANG VIA WIKIMEDIA COMMONS)

BELOW: The naval variant of the 61-K 37mm anti-aircraft gun. (GOVERNMENT OF THE RUSSIAN FEDERATION VIA WIKIMEDIA COMMONS)

By the mid-1930s, Soviet engineers had become aware of the proliferation and performance of the Swedish-built Bofors 40mm gun. In response, they undertook a design of their own, adapted to Soviet industrial capabilities and specifications. The K-61 37mm anti-aircraft gun was the result, utilised both by Red Army land forces and with the Soviet Navy throughout World War Two. By 1938, Artillery Factory No 8 in Sverdlovsk had received orders to develop the gun under the auspices of chief designer Mikhail Loginov and supervisor Lev Loktev. Tests were undertaken by the autumn of that year and the 61-K entered service in 1939.

Firing from a single barrel that stretched 8ft, 2in, the K-61 weighed 4,600lb. It was often mounted atop a four-wheel ZU-7 carriage with the wheels lifted off the ground and the firing platform supported by screw jacks at its front and rear, as well as two outrigger points. The weapon was fed by five-round clips loaded into the magazine for a continuous

rate of fire as the gunner inserted the next clip just as the previous was expended. The 61-K utilised hydrospring recoil and could be elevated to a maximum of 85° in its Red Army variant for use against low flying enemy aircraft. It was often towed by light trucks such as the GAZ-63.

On the Eastern Front, the 61-K was often effective against Luftwaffe Ju-87 Stuka dive bombers and strafing fighters. A total of 200 ready rounds were carried with each gun. The 61-K could be depressed to -5° as a field weapon and was effective against enemy light armoured fighting vehicles and troop concentrations with a muzzle velocity of 900ft per second.

The 61-K remained in Red Army service after World War Two and was an influential design for future light guns. It appeared in later conflicts with communist forces in Southeast Asia.

61-K 37mm	
Country of Origin	Soviet Union
Calibre	37mm
Crew	8
Range	22,000 feet altitude
Rate of Fire	160 rounds per minute
Number manufactured	20,000

Type 3 120mm

Defending the Home Islands

The US Army Air Force's bombing campaign against the home islands of Japan during World War Two has been a subject of great interest through the ensuing decades. Heavy Boeing B-29 Superfortress bombers rained destruction on Japanese cities, igniting firestorms and devastating the country's industrial base, while inflicting massive casualties.

In addition to fighter interceptors, one of the primary Japanese defensive weapons against the big US bombers was the Type 3 120mm anti-aircraft gun. Named for its year of acceptance by the Japanese military – 2603 according to the ancient calendar – the weapon entered production in 1943 as the army's only gun fielded with powered rather than manual controls and with power ramming and semi-automated fuze setting incorporated into the loading tray.

The Type 3 was intended as a replacement for the Type 88 75mm gun that lacked the range to take on four-engined aircraft at high altitude. The Army Technical Bureau developed the gun with a sliding breech and hydropneumatic recoil system. It was configured with a centralised pedestal mount supported by a five-legged firing platform that was anchored with adjustable ground screws for stability and enhanced gun levelling capabilities. The weapon was fed by a pair of magazines situated on an oscillating mount within the turret, each of them holding 52 rounds of ammunition.

The Type 3 weighed more than 43,600lb. Its single barrel was 20ft long and the gun fired at a maximum elevation of 90° with a muzzle velocity of 2,800ft per second. In action, the Type 93 proved one of the few Japanese anti-aircraft guns capable of engaging the B-29s. However, Japanese industry was incapable of producing it in sufficient numbers to impact the course of the air war.

The few available were usually deployed to protect Japanese cities or installations that were vital to the war effort, such as steel mills and oil fields and reserves.

Records indicate that one unit of Type 3 120mm anti-aircraft guns that protected the Japanese capital city of Tokyo was credited with shooting down 10 B-29s.

ABOVE: Type 3 120mm anti-aircraft gun atop a heavy six-wheel trailer. (GOVERNMENT OF JAPAN IMPERIAL JAPANESE ARMY VIA WIKIMEDIA COMMONS)

LEFT: Type 3 120mm anti-aircraft gun at a firing range in Japan. (GOVERNMENT OF JAPAN IMPERIAL JAPANESE ARMY VIA WIKIMEDIA COMMONS)

LEFT: The imposing 20ft barrel of a Type 3 120mm. (CREATIVE COMMONS DORICONO VIA WIKIMEDIA COMMONS)

Type 3 120mm	
Country of Origin	Japan
Calibre	120mm
Crew	13
Range	66,000 feet altitude
Rate of Fire	20 rounds per minute
Number manufactured	157

Ordnance QF 3.7-inch

Firing an 84mm shell that weighed 28 pounds, the Ordnance QF (quick firing) 3.7-inch anti-aircraft gun was the standard weapon of its type in British service throughout World War Two. Intended to defend against high altitude enemy bomber formations, it has been compared to other heavy guns such as the US 90mm and German 88mm types.

The origin of the QF 3.7-inch dates to the late 1920s and the realisation that air power was on the ascendancy based on the experience of World War One. Vickers-Armstrong developed a prototype in response to stated specifications in 1928, but development was slow due to post-war financial constraints. The QF 3.7-inch gun was not put through trials and accepted for production until 1936. General production began the following year and steadily increased with the prospects of renewed conflict with Germany.

The 3.7-inch gun replaced older 3-inch models in heavy anti-aircraft batteries of the Royal Artillery. It was acknowledged as being somewhat ponderous with a weight of 20,541lb. Its barrel length stretched 15ft, 5in, and it operated using a horizontal sliding wedge breech block and hydropneumatic recoil. It was emplaced in static mounts and configured for mobile deployment atop the four-wheeled carriage Mk I or Mk III, with four folding outrigger legs and levelling jacks. Its maximum elevation was 80°, and it was deemed highly effective in its primary role. In the field, the weapon was sometimes pressed into service as standard field artillery or an anti-tank gun. However, in the latter it was less than optimal due to its significant weight, although it could be depressed to -5° to fire at ground targets.

The QF 3.7-inch gun made its combat debut with the opening months of World War Two in 1939 and was a key element of air defence during the Battle of Britain. From September 1939 to the autumn of 1940, the number of guns deployed increased from 540 to 1,140 and production stepped up to more than 200 per month.

Deployed in large numbers around British cities and prominent military installations during the Battle of Britain, the QF 3.7-inch gun performed well. It was also deployed in the China-Burma-India theatre, North Africa, Italy and western Europe. Manufactured in Britain, Australia, and Canada, it improved during the war years in subsequent marks and remained in service for decades up to the present day.

Ordnance Qf 3.7-inch	
Country of Origin	Great Britain
Calibre	3.7-inch (84mm)
Crew	7
Range	45,000 feet altitude
Rate of Fire	10 rounds per minute
Number manufactured	10,000

Self-propelled Artillery

Armour, Firepower and Mobility

Perhaps haunted by the memory of trench warfare and the horrendous casualties sustained on the Western Front during World War One, the planners of military operations were determined that the renewed conflict of 1939-1945 would be one of mobile warfare rather than stalemate.

In addition to the desire to avoid prolonged battlefield stagnation, the military establishments of the major powers understood the devastating capability of artillery, which had inflicted the majority of land casualties in World War One, and intended to harness its firepower to keep pace with infantry and armoured units in a war of movement.

Thus, the concept of self-propelled artillery came to the fore during the years between the world wars. Towed artillery was powerful, but it was cumbersome and always a challenge to transport and deploy, particularly cross country. Further, towed artillery took time to place into firing position and was vulnerable to enemy counter battery fire or air attack once its position was found and fixed by enemy forces. Theoretically, a more mobile form of artillery could keep pace with advancing formations, deliver supporting direct or indirect fire, relocate rapidly and contribute to the momentum of an attack at critical points.

The British Army had actually experimented with the concept of self-propelled artillery during World War One with the Gun Carrier Mk I, a BL 5-inch gun or 6-inch howitzer mounted on the chassis of a Mk I tank. With the principle established, it was no great leap to incorporate artillery with the tank chassis as armour also evolved through the 1930s.

While the gun and howitzer were combined with the tank to achieve better overall battlefield performance, the addition of armour allowed for higher crew survivability and self-propelled artillery became a standard component of land warfare. The German blitzkrieg employed self-propelled artillery in its lightning ground advance and all major warring powers initiated such weapons to provide the flexible support of big guns.

During World War Two, a number of self-propelled artillery models were developed and deployed. Among these were the German Wespe and Hummel, the British Bishop and Sexton, the US Priest and the Soviet ISU-122 and ISU-152.

M7 105mm Priest

The US Army recognised the requirement for a mobile artillery piece early in World War Two and addressed the need with the M7 105mm howitzer motor carriage. Because of its high-mounted machine gun ring, the vehicle was nicknamed 'Priest' by British soldiers who used it.

The M7 underwent trials and was accepted for production from the prototype T32 in February 1942. Within weeks, the programme was underway as the British Army requested a whopping 2,500 of the vehicles at a critical time in the war in North Africa. A total of 4,400 were ordered for delivery by the end of 1943, but such numbers were never achieved.

The M7 Priest was first used in combat by British troops during the Battle of El Alamein in October 1942, alongside the British Bishop self-propelled gun that mounted the Ordnance QF 25-pounder. US armoured divisions were supplied with three battalions of M7s, while the British 3rd and 50th Divisions and the Canadian 3rd Division were issued the weapon in the 1944 drive toward the German frontier from Normandy. Allied forces also used the M7 in the Pacific, where it provided a significant boost to the British and Commonwealth 14th Army during the 1945 offensive that captured Meiktila, Mandalay and Rangoon while driving the Japanese out of Burma.

The M7 remained in service through the Korean War and was utilised by Israeli forces in the Six-Day War of 1967 and the 1973 Yom Kippur War. The West German Bundeswehr also fielded the weapon during the Cold War, and it was constructed in at least half-a-dozen variants.

Over time, the M7 was manufactured by the American Locomotive Company, Federal Machine and Welder and Pressed Steel Car. The initial combination of the M1 or M2 105mm howitzer was with the chassis of an M3 Lee tank, but with the increasing availability of the M4 Sherman tank chassis, production later switched to that platform. The M7 stood 8ft, 4in tall and was capable of a top speed of 24mph on improved roads or 15mph cross country. It was powered by the nine-cylinder Continental R-975 radial petrol engine generating up to 400hp. Secondary armament included a single Browning M2 .50-calibre machine gun.

M7 Priest 105mm	
Country of Origin	United States
Calibre	105mm
Crew	8
Range	120 miles
Engine	Continental R-975 radial petrol
Number manufactured	4,316

M40 155mm & M12 155mm

Long Tom on Tracks

The US Army's M40 155mm gun motor carriage was indicative of the continuing evolution of self-propelled artillery that took place during World War Two. The M40 developed from the prototype T83 that mounted the 155mm M1A1 or M2 155mm 'Long Tom' field gun atop the wider and longer chassis of the M4 Sherman medium tank.

Powered by the 340hp Wright R-975 Whirlwind engine, which was also built by Continental under license, the M40 was capable of a top speed of 24mph on improved roads and 14mph cross country, with a range of 106 miles. Its prototype T83 was officially designated M40 when the vehicle entered production in 1944. The M40 was produced in 1944 and 1945 by the Pressed Steel Car Company and saw only limited action in World War Two with the 991st Field Artillery Battalion on the Western Front. A total of 24 were converted to the M43 howitzer motor carriage mounting an 8in weapon.

The M40 was intended as the successor to the M12 gun motor carriage, which mounted a US derivative of the French Canon de 155mm GPF field gun. The M12 was promoted for evaluation by 1941 and the prototype T6 gun motor carriage

ABOVE: The M40 155mm Gun Motor Carriage is preserved at Aberdeen Proving Ground, Maryland. (CREATIVE COMMONS MARK PELLEGRINI VIA WIKIMEDIA COMMONS)

LEFT: An M12 155mm fires in support of the Moselle River crossing in France, 1944. (NATIONAL ARCHIVES AND RECORDS ADMINISTRATION VIA WIKIMEDIA COMMONS)

was put through trials in early 1942, with an initial production order for 100 accepted into service in March 1943.

Constructed on the chassis of an M3 Lee tank, the M12 stood just over 9ft, 5in high. It was also powered by a variant of the Wright R-975 engine with a maximum speed of 24mph. Its vertical volute suspension was typical of American armoured vehicles of the World War Two period. It weighed 59,000lb and was manufactured by the Pressed Steel Car Company.

Initially, the M12 was utilised in training. However, prior to the D-Day landings in Normandy on June 6, 1944, more than 70 were made ready for combat operations with six armoured field artillery battalions. These were regularly in service during the Normandy campaign and beyond, being effective in providing both indirect field artillery support or reducing fixed

fortifications, particularly during assaults against German strongpoints along the Siegfried Line or West Wall. The M12 earned the nicknames of 'Doorknocker' or 'King Kong' from its crews due to its ability to fire armour piercing shells that could penetrate an estimated seven-foot thickness of concrete.

BELOW: M12 155mm self-propelled gun at the US Army Artillery Museum, Fort Sill, Oklahoma. (CREATIVE COMMONS FRELON420 VIA WIKIMEDIA COMMONS)

M40 & M12 155mm	
Country of Origin	United States
Calibre	155mm
Crew	8; 6
Range	106 miles; 140 miles
Rate of Fire	1 round per minute; 3 rounds per minute
Number manufactured	418; 100

sIG 33 PzKpfw I Bison

A Rolling Rampart

ABOVE: This Bison and its alert crew were photographed in Russia in 1942. (CREATIVE COMMONS BUNDESARCHIV BILD VIA WIKIMEDIA COMMONS)

RIGHT: A Bison in the field in Greece in the spring of 1941. (CREATIVE COMMONS BUNDESARCHIV BILD VIA WIKIMEDIA COMMONS)

The 150mm sIG 33 heavy infantry gun, developed in the late 1920s, gradually transitioned from its original support role to arm a family of self-propelled artillery vehicles of the German Army before and during World War Two. The gun remained in production from 1936 through the end of the war, and no fewer than five self-propelled artillery vehicles mounted the powerful weapon.

Perhaps the most prominent among these was the 150mm sIG 33 (Sf) PzKpfw I Ausf B, nicknamed 'Bison'. This vehicle paired the sIG 33 atop the modified chassis of a Panzer I tank and was effectively among the first vehicles of its type in the German wartime arsenal. The Bison evolved following the German invasion of Poland in 1939 as it was determined that towed versions of the sIG 33, which weighed about 4,000lb, were unable to keep pace with the racing armoured spearheads that characterised the Nazi blitzkrieg.

As a result, an immediate attempt was made to mount the sIG 33 atop the Panzer I chassis with complete carriage and wheels. Armour was added, presenting a tall, 'fortified' look that raised the height of the somewhat improvised fighting vehicle to 9ft, 2in. Ammunition stowage was impossible in the cramped firing compartment, requiring replenishment to take place from an accompanying vehicle. In addition, the high silhouette made it vulnerable to enemy fire. The Bison weighed 18,800lb and its six-cylinder Maybach NL38 petrol engine produced a top speed of 25mph on the road.

A relative few of the Bisons were configured for combat as its drawbacks were apparent. Instead, independent self-propelled heavy infantry gun companies were organised after the conversion of 38 vehicles in February 1940. These Bisons were deployed to the Balkans and saw action during Operation Barbarossa, the Nazi invasion of the Soviet Union on June 22, 1941. The last of these is thought to have been in battle in mid-1943.

The sIG 150mm infantry gun was also mounted on the modified chassis of the Panzer II and III, the Czech-built Panzer 38(t) and the Hetzer modified chassis.

RIGHT: A rare surviving Bison in service with Israeli forces in 1948. (NATIONAL LIBRARY OF ISRAEL VIA WIKIMEDIA COMMONS)

sIG 33 PzKpfw I Bison	
Country of Origin	Germany
Calibre	150mm
Crew	4
Range	87 miles
Rate of Fire	2 rounds per minute
Number manufactured	38

105mm Wespe & 150mm Hummel

Sting of Wasp and Bumblebee

Combat experience convinced the German Army high command that its towed field artillery and its early Panzer I and II tanks were inadequate to support or spearhead further offensive action. In addition to the development of heavier tanks, the Germans sought to provide mobile indirect fire support for the panzer divisions in the form of self-propelled artillery.

Two examples of the design effort that ensued were the Leichte Feldhaubitze 18/2 auf Fahrgestell PzKpfw II, popularly known as the Wespe (Wasp), and the Panzer Feldhaubitze 18M auf Geschützwagen III/IV, nicknamed Hummel (Bumblebee). The Wespe mounted an 105mm leFH 18 howitzer, while the Hummel was armed with an 150mm sFH 18 howitzer. The two designs were basically undertaken in tandem and utilised components that were readily available.

The Wespe basically mounted the 105mm howitzer to a PzKpfw II chassis. Modifications to accommodate the rear mounted weapon included moving the engine toward the centre of the vehicle and lengthening the overall structure. Light armour was placed atop the chassis but afforded little more than protection against small arms. The open top made the vehicle vulnerable to air attack and shrapnel from exploding shells. The Wespe weighed 24,250lb and was powered by the six-cylinder Maybach HL62 petrol engine with a maximum speed of 25mph. Dedicated production began in February 1943 and concluded in June 1944 when Soviet forces approached the manufacturing facility in Warsaw, Poland. On the battlefield, the Wespe performed well in its 1943 debut on the Eastern Front and Panzer II chassis production was solely allocated to it afterward.

Like the Wespe, the Hummel was designed in 1942, but it was paired with a modified variant of the PzKpfw III and IV chassis. An early 150mm gun was discarded in favour of the more powerful sFH 18, while the chassis was modified with the engine in the centre to make room for the weapon to be mounted at the rear. Other internal modifications were later made for driver and radio operator space. The Hummel entered combat

in 1943 at the Battle of Kursk on the Eastern Front, serving in armoured artillery battalions attached to the panzer divisions. It was powered by the V-12 petrol Maybach HL120 engine with a top speed of 26mph. It was open-topped like the Wespe, therefore also susceptible to air attack and exploding shells, with limited protection for its crew.

Although produced in relatively low numbers, both the Wespe and Hummel served in Italy and western Europe.

Wespe 105mm & Hummel 150mm	
Country of Origin	Germany
Calibre	105mm; 150mm
Crew	5; 6
Range	137 miles; 133 miles
Rate of Fire	4 rounds per minute; 2 rounds per minute
Number manufactured	676; 714

LEFT: This 105mm Wespe was destroyed in action during the Normandy campaign of 1944. (NATIONAL ARCHIVES AND RECORDS ADMINISTRATION VIA WIKIMEDIA COMMONS)

BELOW: A battery of 150mm Hummels supporting an attack on the Eastern Front in the summer of 1943. (CREATIVE COMMONS BUNDESARCHIV BILD VIA WIKIMEDIA COMMONS)

Sturmgeschutz III

RIGHT: German soldiers manoeuvre in Russia with a StuG III in close support. (CREATIVE COMMONS BUNDESARCHIV BILD VIA WIKIMEDIA COMMONS)

The cost of manufacturing weapons of war has long been one of the limiting factors in production and such was the case in Nazi Germany. Known for high quality, precision weaponry, the German military nevertheless felt the constraints of expense as World War Two dragged on, while the need for armoured fighting vehicles only increased. One solution to the expense associated with turreted tanks was the Sturmgeschütz III (StuG III), a turretless assault gun that functioned as infantry support artillery and tank destroyer. The StuG III was comparatively economical and eventually was produced in greater numbers than any other German armoured fighting vehicle of the conflict.

The result of a proposal first put forward by General Erich von Manstein in the mid-1930s, the impetus for the StuG III was not only in cost savings but in the conclusion that mobile German infantry and armoured formations needed direct fire support in the field.

Daimler Benz AG developed the StuG III from the chassis of a PzKpfw III medium tank with the Krupp-built 75mm short barrel StuK 37 L/24 main gun, and five prototypes were introduced for trials by 1937. The first production variant, 'ausf A', entered service in 1940 prior to the

RIGHT: Sturmgeschütz III mounting the 75mm gun of a late variant. (COLLECTIONS OF THE IMPERIAL WAR MUSEUMS VIA WIKIMEDIA COMMONS)

BELOW: Sturmgeschütz III with a short barrel 75mm gun crosses a river on the Eastern Front in October 1941. (NATIONAL DIGITAL ARCHIVES OF POLAND VIA WIKIMEDIA COMMONS)

invasion of France and the Low Countries. During the course of World War Two the vehicle was built in at least seven variants. Following combat experience on the Eastern Front, the StuG III was upgunned with a long barrel 75mm gun with greater muzzle velocity. By December 1943, the StuG IV, built on the chassis of the PzKpfw IV medium tank, had been developed.

The StuG III weighed 52,690lb and stood just over 7ft high. Its low silhouette improved concealment on the battlefield and made the weapon ideal for ambush. Powered by the 296hp Maybach HL 120 petrol engine, it was capable of a top speed of 25mph. The significant disadvantage of a turretless armoured vehicle was the lack of traverse, which made the

StuG III more vulnerable to attack from flank and rear. Further, its utility was limited in the confines of urban warfare as narrow streets restricted movement and field of fire. Secondary armament included a pair of 7.92mm MG34 or MG42 machine guns.

The Sturmhaubitze III was a notable variant armed with an 105mm howitzer.

Sturmgeschütz III	
Country of Origin	Germany
Calibre	75mm
Crew	4
Range	96 miles
Rate of Fire	8 rounds per minute
Number manufactured	10,000

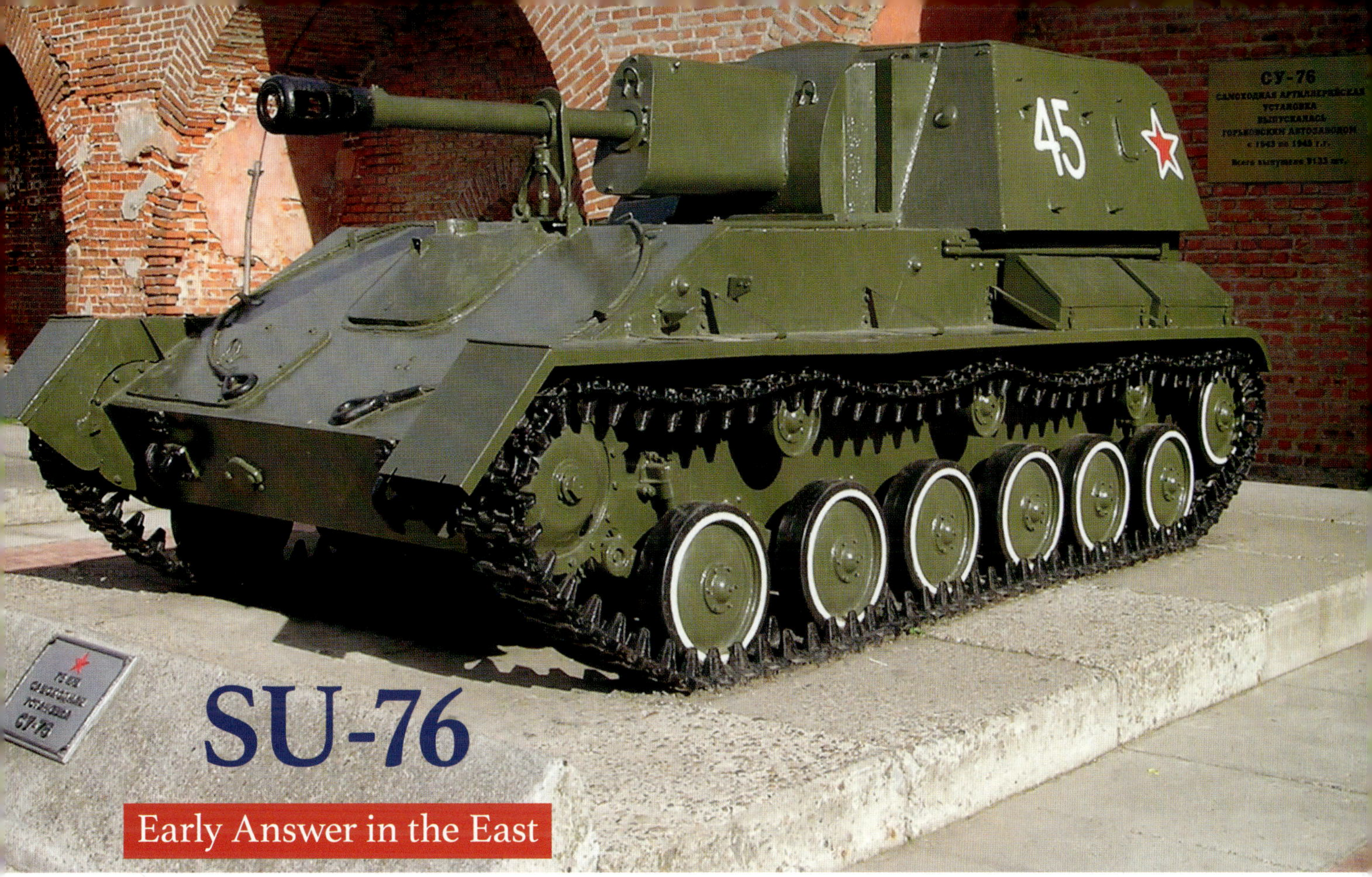

SU-76

Early Answer in the East

Early combat revealed to Soviet military commanders the weaknesses of their T-60 and T-70 light tanks, which were susceptible even to light anti-tank fire during Operation Barbarossa, the German invasion of the Soviet Union on June 22, 1941. Their solution was to augment Red Army armoured formations with a versatile self-propelled gun, either the ZiS-3 or ZiS-76, mounted atop the chassis of a T-70 in an infantry support and anti-tank role.

The design of the SU-76 began in mid-1942 under the direction of SA Ginzburg. The vehicle was soon accepted for service, and production began by early December. By mid-1943, the SU-76 was appearing on the battlefield in substantial numbers. The hull of the T-70 was lengthened to accommodate the rear mounting of a 76mm ZiS-3 field gun and additional road wheels were introduced. The 37th and 38th factories of the GAZ Automobile Works in Gorki were fully engaged in manufacturing the SU-76 by early 1943.

The initial powerplant was the six-cylinder GAZ 202 petrol engine, but this was deemed insufficient and exhibited maintenance issues in the field. Subsequent production models were powered by the 84hp GAZ 203, which achieved a top speed of 27mph. The vehicle was open-topped, making it vulnerable to bursting artillery shells and air attack. Little attention was paid to the comfort of the crew and the fighting compartment was cramped, prompting its crewmen to dub their vehicle 'The Bitch'. However, it did render outstanding service during the course of the Great Patriotic War.

As the Germans introduced their powerful PzKpfw V Panther medium and PzKpfw VI Tiger heavy tanks, the 76mm ZiS gun was rendered inferior in tank-vs-tank combat due to its limited range. As the SU-85, with a heavier weapon, came into production, the SU-76 was increasingly tasked with direct infantry support. It was adept at hitting enemy fixed strongpoints and troop concentrations, while its light weight added mobility in the field. Its relatively low cost allowed prolific construction and, by the end of World War Two, only the legendary T-34 medium tank had been produced in greater numbers.

SU-76	
Country of Origin	Soviet Union
Calibre	76mm
Crew	4
Range	160 miles
Rate of Fire	10 rounds per minute
Number manufactured	14,292

ABOVE: SU-76 self-propelled artillery gun on display in Nizhny Novgorod, Russia. (CREATIVE COMMONS LOSTARTILLERYMAN VIA WIKIMEDIA COMMONS)

LEFT: An SU-76 alongside an M26 Pershing heavy tank during the Korean War. (US MARINE CORPS VIA WIKIMEDIA COMMONS)

BELOW: The SU-76 was a mainstay of Red Army infantry support during the Great Patriotic War. (CREATIVE COMMONS CMAPM VIA WIKIMEDIA COMMONS)

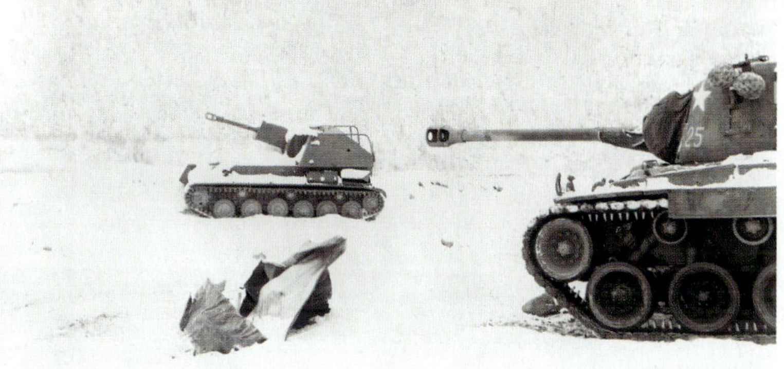

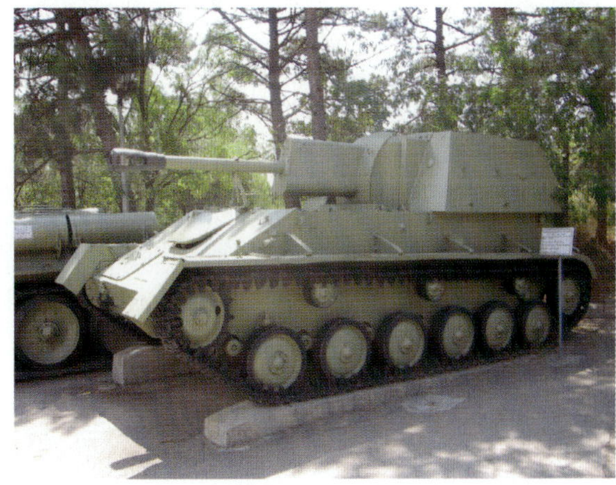

ISU-122 & ISU-152

Upgunned Tank and Troop Hunters

RIGHT: The prototype ISU-122 shown as the self-propelled weapon entered production. (CREATIVE COMMONS DENNIS KOVACIK VIA WIKIMEDIA COMMONS)

The Soviet Red Army placed significant emphasis on the tank destroyer, self-propelled artillery and infantry support weaponry that came to symbolize its surge across Eastern Europe and into Berlin during the Great Patriotic War. The introduction of the SU-76 and SU-122 provided great service as the Red Army seized the initiative on the Eastern Front. However, with the introduction of heavier German tanks came the realisation that heavier weapons were needed to counter them. At the same time, Red Army infantry and armoured formations encountered stiff German resistance at fortress cities that Adolf Hitler had decreed should be held at all costs.

The Soviets researched and developed more powerful self-propelled artillery by the end of 1943. The prototype of the ISU-122 married the 122mm A-19 gun with the chassis of an IS-2 (Josef Stalin) heavy tank. The Soviet State Defence Committee authorised the production of the ISU-122 in March 1944, with the first of these vehicles emergin from the Chelyabinsk Kirov factory, nicknamed 'Tankograd', just a month later. The ISU-122 with modifications remained in production through the end of 1945.

In later variants the A-19 gun was replaced by the D-25, but the original armament continued in manufacture of the ISU-122 due to its availability.

The ISU-122 weighed just over 50 tonnes and was powered by the 520hp V-21S diesel engine producing a top speed of 23mph. Its secondary armament consisted of a 12.7mm DShK anti-aircraft machine gun. It was used extensively on the Eastern Front, primarily in infantry and anti-tank support as the heavier ISU-152 was preferred in urban warfare settings.

The ISU-152 shared many of the characteristics of the ISU-122. It was fully enclosed for crew protection, although the interior of the self-propelled weapon was tight. It mounted the 152mm ML-20S gun howitzer. Although it was initially expected to fill the anti-tank and infantry support roles, it was found to be an exceptionally adept tank destroyer as well. On the battlefield, it earned the nickname 'Beast Killer'.

The prototype ISU-152 was unveiled in January 1943, moving from the chassis of the IS-1 to the IS-2 heavy tank. It was surprisingly mobile for its weight of more than 52 tonnes and possessed a top speed of 19mph supplied by the same 12-cylinder V-21S petrol engine as the ISU-122. Secondary armament included the .50-calibre DShK machine gun. The sledgehammer weapon was deployed in urban warfare settings in major cities across Eastern Europe and into Germany. It remained in service with numerous Soviet client states into the 1980s.

RIGHT: An ISU-152 self-propelled gun takes part in a military parade in the Ukrainian capital of Kiev. (GOVERNMENT OF THE RUSSIAN FEDERATION VIA WIKIMEDIA COMMONS)

ISU-122 & ISU-152	
Country of Origin	Soviet Union
Calibre	122mm; 152mm
Crew	4; 4
Range	140 miles; 137 miles
Rate of Fire	2 rounds per minute; 2 rounds per minute
Number manufactured	2,410; 4,635

RIGHT: Red Army soldiers ride atop the ISU-152 during a rapid advance toward the frontier of Germany. (GOVERNMENT OF THE RUSSIAN FEDERATION VIA WIKIMEDIA COMMONS)

Sexton

Mobile 25-Pounder Weapon

Mobile artillery support was crucial during a war of movement and, in World War Two, the British General Staff sought a suitable self-propelled mount for its Ordnance QF 25-pounder gun. The Valentine tank chassis was paired with the gun to produce the Bishop armoured fighting vehicle with less than optimal results, while the American M7 Priest was ordered in numbers that could never be met from a production standpoint.

Meanwhile, inquiries with the Canadian government prompted that nation's Army Engineering Design Branch and the Canadian Department of Munitions to take up a design programme. The result was the prototype Sexton, nicknamed for the church's traditional religious custodian, in keeping with other self-propelled guns such as the Bishop and Deacon. The Sexton was built atop the Canadian-manufactured

Ram tank, a variant of the chassis of the American M3 Lee/Grant, with the 25-pounder as its main weapon. Eventually, the Sexton I was produced using the M3 chassis, while the Sexton II was built with the 'Grizzly' chassis of the US M4 Sherman medium tank.

The modified M3 chassis and 25-pounder prototype emerged in June 1943 and the Montreal Locomotive Works set to production of an initial order of 124 vehicles. The Sexton was placed in service in the spring of 1943. It weighed 25 tonnes and was powered by the 400hp nine-cylinder

Sexton	
Country of Origin	Canada
Calibre	25-pounder (87.6mm)
Crew	6
Range	125 miles
Rate of Fire	6 rounds per minute
Number manufactured	2,150

Continental R-975 radial petrol engine producing a top speed of 25mph. Its crew compartment was armoured for protection against small-arms fire and shell fragments, but open-topped. A pair of .303-inch Bren light machine guns provided secondary armament for defence against enemy infantry and aircraft.

The Sexton first saw combat with the British Eighth Army in Italy in the autumn of 1943, providing the mobility and firepower desired in support of infantry and armoured formations in rugged terrain. Its indirect fire role was supplemented by the ability to take on enemy strongpoints and fixed fortifications. During the D-Day landings, Sexton vehicles came ashore with Commonwealth troops, firing their guns against German positions even before they rolled off their landing craft onto the invasion beaches.

The Sexton remained in service with Commonwealth forces into the mid-1950s.

ABOVE: Sexton guns of the Hertfordshire Yeomanry open fire against German positions in April 1945. (COLLECTIONS OF THE IMPERIAL WAR MUSEUMS VIA WIKIMEDIA COMMONS)

BELOW LEFT: A Sexton rumbles through a shattered French village during the fighting in northwestern Europe, August 1944. (COLLECTIONS OF THE IMPERIAL WAR MUSEUMS VIA WIKIMEDIA COMMONS)

BELOW RIGHT: A Canadian-built Sexton self-propelled artillery piece crosses the River Seine in Normandy. (COLLECTIONS OF THE IMPERIAL WAR MUSEUMS VIA WIKIMEDIA COMMONS)

Bishop

Irreverent Weapon on Tracks

The experience of combat in North Africa exposed the lack of mobility in the artillery formations of the British and Commonwealth forces that battled Panzerarmee Afrika. In a rushed attempt to bring such capability to the field, the British military establishment relied on the Birmingham Railway Carriage and Wagon Company to develop its first real self-propelled artillery weapon of World War Two.

The Bishop, so named because its high superstructure necessary to house the Ordnance QF 25-pounder gun resembled the mitre headwear of the church official, was developed in the summer of 1941, with the prototype accepted and ordered into production by November. The armoured fighting vehicle paired the 25-pounder with the chassis of a Valentine II tank and the British Army placed its first order for 100.

The design of the Bishop was flawed from the beginning, with its sheer size and superstructure presenting an inviting target to enemy gunners in the open desert. The vehicle was cumbersome, with an enclosed superstructure that featured heavy rear doors for crew ingress and egress. Additionally, the modifications to the tank hull and required configuration to accommodate the 25-pounder resulted in a maximum gun elevation that was limited to only 15°, while the gun could be depressed to -5°. As a result, it was often difficult for the

Bishop to accomplish indirect fire support missions, causing the crews to utilise natural embankments or even to construct ramps to raise the firing angle sufficiently.

The Bishop's ponderous weight at 38,580lb and its slow speed further hampered its performance. Powered by the 131hp AEC A190 diesel engine, it could manage only 15mph at top speed. The Bishop stood 10ft high. It saw action for the first time at the Battle of El Alamein in October 1942, as well as during the Italian campaign. However, its shortcomings spelled its demise, soon to be replaced by the US-built M7 Priest and the much improved Canadian Sexton.

Bishop	
Country of Origin	Great Britain
Calibre	25-pounder (87.6mm)
Crew	4
Range	90 miles
Rate of Fire	3 rounds per minute
Number manufactured	149

Mountain Artillery

Thunder on High Ground

Artillery is a valuable resource on the modern battlefield, whenever and wherever it may be deployed. Given its influence on the open plains, deserts and forests, perhaps the greatest challenge to artillery on land is mountainous terrain, which is treacherous and difficult for the soldier to traverse with only his personal weapon and essential gear. Nevertheless, the concept of mountain artillery has been around for some time, although its existence as a subset of field artillery in general came to the fore principally in the latter half of the 19th Century.

During the American Civil War, weapons described as mountain howitzers were wrestled into position on high ground and, by the 1890s, campaigns across the mountain ranges of Europe had brought greater emphasis to the idea that lightweight artillery that could be broken down into components that were man portable or could strapped to the backs of pack animals and then reassembled for action might tip the balance in battle.

During World War One, both the Allies and Central Powers utilised mountain artillery and the fighting between Italian and Austrian troops in the rugged Dolomites and Julian Alps

proved its worth. A generation later in World War Two, the major powers had devoted resources to the development of light artillery that might be used not only by alpine or mountain troops, but also in an airborne role, adding firepower in support of otherwise lightly armed soldiers, while putting heavier punch in places that might otherwise have been out of reach.

Mountain artillery devolved out of necessity into lighter calibre, smaller and shorter ranged weapons. Their entire assembly had to be

functional, while their ammunition transport added another aspect to the deployment. During World War Two, light mountain artillery found its place with airborne troops, while it was instrumental in the support role during the Italian campaign, the fighting in the Balkans and the struggle in Western Europe from 1944.

Common types of mountain artillery are sometimes classified as field guns or airborne guns/ howitzers and these labels are indicative of their functionality. Such types as the US M1 75mm pack howitzer, the German 75mm Gebirgsgeschütz 36 and Gebirgsgeschzütz 40, the British QF 3.7-inch mountain howitzer and the Italian Cannone da 65/17 were commonly in service.

ABOVE: German soldiers guiding pack animals loaded with mountain artillery components during World War One. (SWISS FEDERAL ARCHIVES VIA WIKIMEDIA COMMONS)

LEFT: German soldiers man their mountain artillery in rugged terrain. Note the spent shells in the foreground. (CREATIVE COMMONS BUNDESARCHIV BILD VIA WIKIMEDIA COMMONS)

LEFT: Australian artillerymen fire their mountain howitzer against Japanese positions in New Guinea. (CREATIVE COMMONS AUSTRALIAN WAR MEMORIAL VIA WIKIMEDIA COMMONS)

Gebirgshaubitze 40 105mm

Rheinmetall and the Mountains

Purpose built to provide more firepower to German mountain units, the Gebirgshaubitze 40 (GebH 40) 105mm mountain howitzer was the heaviest weapon of its type fielded during World War Two, capably filling its assigned role to augment the punch of the 75mm Gebirgsgeschutz 36 mountain gun.

The GebH 40 was the product of a design competition between arms manufacturers Rheinmetall and Austria/Böhler. The two companies submitted prototypes based on military specifications in 1940 and the Böhler design was chosen after extensive field trials. Production was delayed for nearly two years but continued into 1945 and the end of the war.

Despite its weight at 3,660lb, the powerful GebH 40 was known for its mobility and ease of deployment. It was constructed so that it could be towed intact by vehicle or towed by the Kettenkrad half-track in four separate trailer loads. When animals were used for transport, its components could be disassembled

into five loads, proving that the initial design focusing on ease of transport was valid.

The GebH 40 utilised a horizontal sliding block breech with hydropneumatic recoil and split trail carriage. The carriage was constructed with solid rubber tyres and light metal alloy wheels while a spring suspension attached to the legs were designed to help dig into a stable firing position with three points of support. The GebH 40 was known for its quick deployment with the three stabilisation points rather than four, which other weapons were known to require, and it fired a high explosive or armour piercing 32-pound shell. Range was determined based on the incremental use of propellant, which was available in up to six stages.

The GebH 40 reached the front lines in 1942 and served with Axis mountain troops in northern Russia and Finland, France, Italy and the Balkans. Its positive attributes contributed to a service life that extended into the 1960s with several European countries.

Gebirgshaubitze 40 105mm	
Country of Origin	Germany
Calibre	105mm
Crew	7
Range	13,806 yards
Rate of Fire	6 rounds per minute
Number manufactured	420

ABOVE: German soldiers operatin the Gebirgshaubitze 40 105mm mountain howitzer in June 1941. (CREATIVE COMMONS BUNDESARCHIV BILD VIA WIKIMEDIA COMMONS)

M1938 76mm Mountain Gun

Skoda Light and Rugged

team led by engineer LI Gorlitsky at Plant No 7 in Leningrad brought sufficient modifications to the weapon to gain acceptance of the M1983.

The M1938 weighed 1,731lb utilising a vertical sliding block breech with hydropneumatic recoil. Its box trail carriage was wheeled with a spring suspension that facilitated rapid movement under vehicle tow, while pack animals could transport the gun in eight loads. Production began in 1939 and, by the eve of Operation Barbarossa, the M1938 was widely distributed within the Red Army artillery structure. Its high angle of elevation at 65° was a distinct advantage in rugged terrain.

ABOVE: Built in Leningrad, this M1938 76mm mountain gun is now a museum piece in Finland. (CREATIVE COMMONS BALCER-COMMONSWIKI VIA WIKIMEDIA COMMONS)

LEFT: The compact breech and apparatus of the M1938 are visible in this view from behind the gun shield. (CREATIVE COMMONS BALCER-COMMONSWIKI VIA WIKIMEDIA COMMONS)

BELOW: The Soviet M1938 76mm mountain gun was known for its high elevation and angle of fire. (CREATIVE COMMONS SIMM VIA WIKIMEDIA COMMONS)

The famous Skoda munitions works in Czechoslovakia played an important part in arming Germany before and during World War Two. Even though Czechoslovakia was swallowed up by Nazi Germany before the commencement of armed hostilities in Europe, the Skoda works had been involved with several countries in the development of an array of arms.

In 1936, Soviet observers visited the Skoda works to assess the merits of the company's S-5 76mm mountain gun. Their impression was favourable and the military requested the Kremlin fund the purchase of the blueprints and specifications for the production of the wapon in their own country. However, the investment requested from Skoda for a quantity of 400 guns with 400,000 rounds of ammunition topped $22 million. Soviet Chief of Supply V Khalepsky advocated for the deal and with the contract the Czechs received the right to produce the Tupolev SB twin engine bomber under license.

The weapon that came to be known in the Red Army as the M1938 76mm mountain gun was the product of a somewhat frustrating development programme in the Soviet Union. Despite the receipt of the Czech documentation, the gun was never produced in its original configuration. Early testing with the initial 7-1 model was disappointing and reported that performance was inferior to that of World War One mountain artillery. A second attempt, the 7-2, was also deemed inadequate. Eventually, the design

M1938 Mountain Gun 76mm	
Country of Origin	Soviet Union
Calibre	76mm
Crew	5
Range	11,504 yards
Rate of Fire	10 rounds per minute
Number manufactured	1,068

Type 94 75mm

European Influence in Japan

the infantry support artillery weapon of choice during World War Two.

Built with a significant degree of European influence, the Type 94 incorporated a sliding breech block that was patterned after German Krupp and French Schneider designs. Its hydropneumatic recoil was also similar to a proven Schneider configuration. The split trail carriage was long and employed spades to stabilise the firing platform while the weapon was supported by a centralised pivot point that allowed for firing with the trails open or closed. Its field performance was marked by rapid deployment, as it could be disassembled and readied for movement in just three to five minutes. Reassembly was regularly accomplished in just 10 minutes.

Eleven pack loads secured to six animals carried the weapon. Alternatively, 18 soldiers could manage the components, depending on the difficulty of the terrain. In treacherous country, the load was sometimes distributed among more than three dozen men. The gun weighed 1,199lb and the heaviest single component weighed 210lb.

The Type 94 75mm gun was used by Japanese troops from 1935 during the fighting in Manchuria, the Second Sino-Japanese War and in the defence of various island fortifications across the empire during World War Two.

ABOVE: The Japanese Type 41 75mm mountain gun was outmoded by the early 1930s. (PUBLIC DOMAIN MAX SMITH VIA WIKIMEDIA COMMONS)

RIGHT: This Type 94 75mm mountain gun is shown with its small gun shield in place. (CREATIVE COMMONS MIKE 1979 RUSSIA VIA WIKIMEDIA COMMONS)

BELOW: This view of the Type 94 mountain gun shows the European-influenced breech and other construction. (NATIONAL ARCHIVES AND RECORDS ADMINISTRATION VIA WIKIMEDIA COMMONS)

The Japanese Army's combat experience during the mid-1930s military adventure in Manchuria revealed the shortcomings of its Type 41 75mm infantry support gun, a license-built copy of the Krupp Model 1908. The weapon was determined to be difficult to transport, while its firepower, accuracy and range were suboptimal. Therefore, by late 1931, the Army Technical Bureau had embarked on a development programme to produce a superior weapon.

The Type 94 75mm mountain gun reached the prototype phase by the following year and production began in 1934. The new gun was named for the year of its acceptance into service – 2594

according to the Japanese calendar. Although the performance of the new Type 94 was praised, plans to re-equip all the army's artillery regiments were constrained by financial concerns and other military priorities in arms and equipment. The gun was intended as a versatile weapon that could be utilised in all terrain and environments, and it did eventually supplant the Type 41 as

Type 94 75mm	
Country of Origin	Japan
Calibre	75mm
Crew	5
Range	7,800 yards
Rate of Fire	2-4 rounds per minute
Number manufactured	1,550

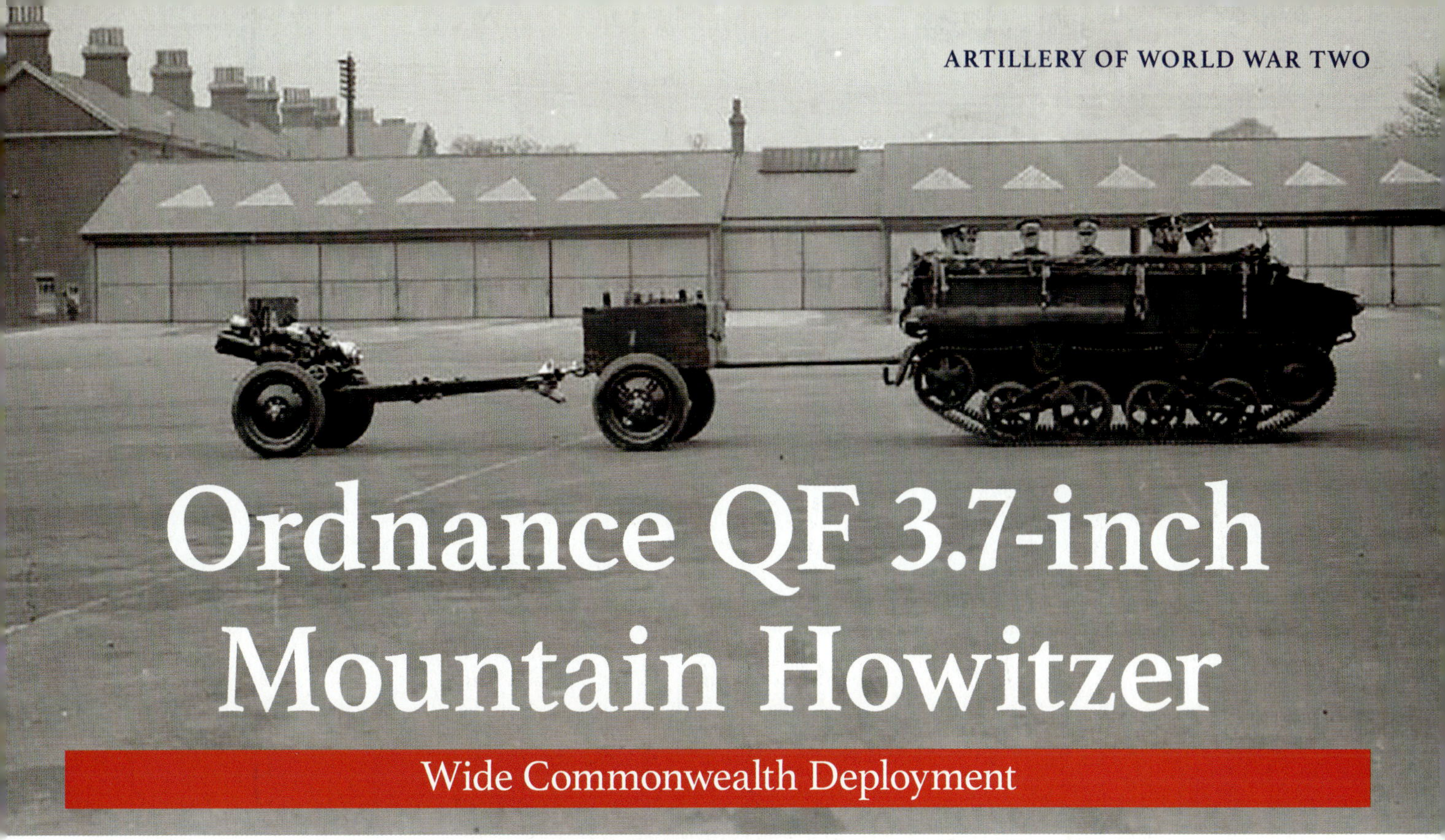

Ordnance QF 3.7-inch Mountain Howitzer

Wide Commonwealth Deployment

Like many other artillery designs of World War Two, the British Ordnance QF 3.7-inch mountain howitzer was a holdover from World War One and its origins stretched back to the early years of the 20th Century, with roots in the Indian subcontinent.

Soldiers of the British Indian Army encountered difficulties with the existing BL 10-pounder mountain gun after it was introduced during the Second Boer War. Its weaknesses included a lack of firepower and a recoil system that required the gun to be returned to firing position after each round was discharged. The 3.7-inch weapon was designed prior to World War One, but delays restricted production until 1915 and deployment with British forces did not come until nearly two years later in December 1916.

The QF (quick firing) 3.7-inch mountain howitzer weighed 1,610lb and fired a variety of shells, the high explosive weighing about 20lb, with an interrupted screw breech and hydropneumatic variable recoil system. Its barrel stretched nearly 4ft and it was secured atop a split trail carriage. The weapon was

disassembled into eight or nine components for transport by pack animals and made its combat debut in East Africa. With an elevation of 40°, it was well suited to warfare in rugged terrain and served in Palestine, as well as Asia. Between the world wars it was utilised by both Indian and British troops along the northwest frontier of India.

During World War Two, the 3.7-inch mountain howitzer was deployed in North Africa and Italy in the European theatre and New Guinea and Burma in the Pacific, while some reports indicate that it was present with New Zealand troops after the desperate fighting on Guadalcanal had subsided in early 1943. It was issued to ground troops and to airborne units as well. British production was augmented during the conflict by factories in India and South Africa.

The howitzer continued in service through the latter half of the 20th Century in Indochina, the Arab-Israeli wars of the 1960s and the Indo-Pakistani wars.

Ordnance QF 3.7-inch Mountain Howitzer	
Country of Origin	Great Britain
Calibre	3.7-inch (94mm)
Crew	6
Range	5,900 yards
Rate of Fire	6 rounds per minute
Number manufactured	183

ABOVE: A QF 3.7-inch mountain howitzer and ammunition trailer being towed by a Dragon artillery tractor. (COLLECTIONS OF THE IMPERIAL WAR MUSEUMS VIA WIKIMEDIA COMMONS)

LEFT: This 3.7-inch mountain howitzer is shown in action against the Japanese in Burma in November 1944. (COLLECTIONS OF THE IMPERIAL WAR MUSEUMS VIA WIKIMEDIA COMMONS)

BELOW: Gunners operate their 3.7-inch mountain howitzer during exercises in Wales, 1942. (COLLECTIONS OF THE IMPERIAL WAR MUSEUMS VIA WIKIMEDIA COMMONS)

Cannone da 65/17

Also known as the Cannone da 65/17 modello 13, this gun was of simple construction and designed for use with infantry and mountain units or alpini of the Italian Army. The designation 65/17 refers to the calibre of 65mm and the length of the barrel at 17 calibres, or 3ft, 7in.

Although it was designed for use with mountain troops, the Cannone da 65/17 was ironically capable of only 20° elevation and intended for low trajectory fire. It weighed 1,225lb, employing a screw-type breech and hydrospring recoil system to fire a shell that weighed 9½lb. The gun could be disassembled for transport by five pack animals and its single arm box trail carriage on two spoked wheels was towed by horses in the field. By the 1920s, it was largely transferred from mountain units to regular infantry formations, gradually replaced by the Czech-built Skoda Model 15 75mm gun, which was renamed Obice da 75/13 in Italian service.

Manufactured by the Royal Arsenal of Naples, the Cannone da 65/17 entered production in 1911 and was in service from 1913 through World War One and saw action in the Spanish Civil War of the mid-1930s. Among other modifications, a folding gun shield was added in 1935 to protect the crew from small-arms fire and shell fragments. In its dual role, it was a close infantry support weapon as well as a mountain gun during World War Two. Mounted on trucks and used as an anti-tank weapon, the Cannone da 65/17 was also used as the main weapon of the Fiat 2000 heavy tank in North Africa.

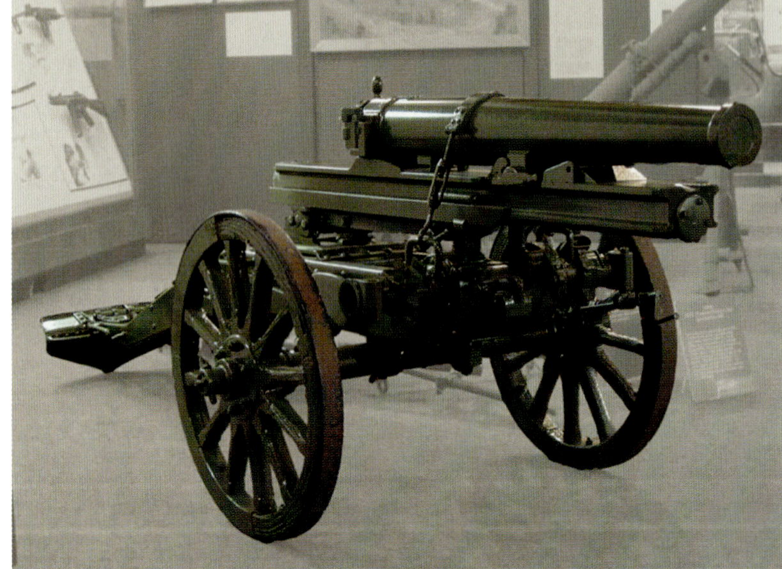

The Cannone da 65/17 was popular with Italian troops throughout its service life because of its light weight and ease of transport. German forces used captured examples after 1943, renaming them the 65mm GebK 246(i). A few guns remained in service after World War Two.

Cannone da 65/17	
Country of Origin	Italy
Crew	6
Calibre	65mm
Range	7,392 yards
Rate of Fire	6 rounds per minute
Number manufactured	720 (approximate)

Rocket Artillery

Next Generation Artillery

The origin of rocket artillery can be traced back to ancient times, as some historians include the fire arrows of the Chinese and their gunpowder-powered projectiles that were used at first as weapons of intimidation but later grew in capability to inflict damage on the enemy.

The rocket continued to develop through the 18th Century as British troops were on the receiving end during the Anglo-Mysore Wars of the late 1700s. The Napoleonic Wars and the War of 1812 saw primitive examples of rocket artillery in action. Notably, Francis Scott Key alluded to the "rockets' red glare" in the US national anthem as he witnessed the bombardment of Fort McHenry by British warships.

Enthusiasm for rocket-powered artillery waned during the late 19th Century as improvements in standard field artillery and heavy guns advanced. However, improvements in the range, firepower and deployment capability of the rocket brought a fresh look at its usefulness in combat by the eve of World War Two. In the opening months of the war in Europe, the German army was already becoming familiar with emerging rocket technology. Development of the famous Nebelwerfer had been undertaken in the 1920s and progressed to the battlefield by 1939.

At the same time, the Soviet armed forces were gaining interest in Katyusha rocket launcher systems. From 1938, the mobile rocket series

had been improved and, by the time of Operation Barbarossa, the Nazi invasion of the Soviet Union on June 22, 1941, the Katyusha truck-mounted rocket launcher was coming into wide use with the Red Army. The US, UK and Japan developed rocket systems of their own, which were used in the Pacific as well as Western Europe.

Rocket artillery during World War Two relied on less accurate weapon systems. However, its merits were rapidly realised. The rocket launchers were mobile, with the ability to fire and displace before

counterbattery fire could zero in on their location. Further, they were capable of delivering saturation bombardment, with a relatively large number of projectiles concentrated in a specific area of enemy activity. In time, these improvements in rocket technology were unleashed, often to devastating effect.

Modern rocket launcher systems are among the foremost types of artillery on the modern battlefield, direct descendants of those developed and deployed before and during World War Two.

Soviet Katyusha rocket launch systems in a Great Patriotic War victory parade in 1945. (MINISTRY OF DEFENCE OF THE RUSSIAN FEDERATION VIA WIKIMEDIA COMMONS)

TOP: German soldiers labour to load a Nebelwerfer multiple rocket launcher on an Italian battlefield in World War Two. (CREATIVE COMMONS BUNDESARCHIV BILD VIA WIKIMEDIA COMMONS)

ABOVE: British soldiers load rockets during the Reichswald offensive in World War Two. (COLLECTIONS OF THE IMPERIAL WAR MUSEUMS VIA WIKIMEDIA COMMONS)

T-34 Calliope 4.5-inch Multiple Rocket Launcher

Missiles to Music

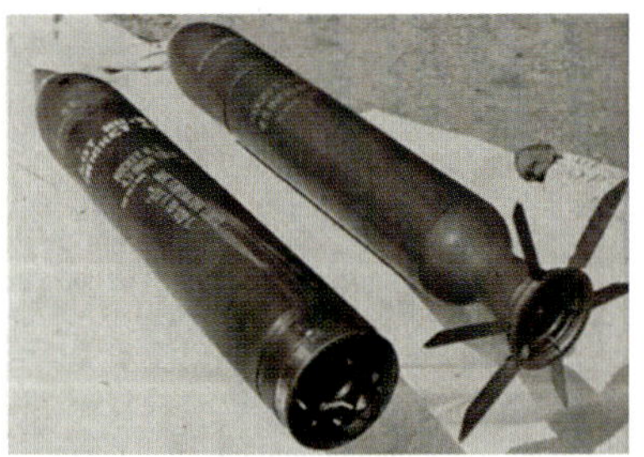

RIGHT: M8 and M16 rockets used with the T-34 Calliope multiple launch rocket system in World War Two. (US ARMY VIA WIKIMEDIA COMMONS)

In anticipation of the fighting that lay ahead in World War Two, the US Army identified a need for enhanced fire support for its ground troops and began experimentation with rocket-powered artillery systems. The T-34 4.5-inch multiple rocket launcher was designed to work in concert with the chassis of the M4 Sherman medium tank to provide that firepower, along with the mobility that efficient cross country movement would require.

The rocket launcher itself consisted of 60 tubes that fired 114mm M8 rockets usually in a saturation or barrage effort against enemy hard targets and strongpoints such as bunkers and pillboxes. The firing tubes were arranged in a bank of 36 tubes permanently affixed atop the M4 chassis with a pair of removable 12-tube banks. The entire rocket apparatus was attached to the sides of the M4 turret by steel beams to the left and right. A pivot point allowed the system to traverse and to fire at an extreme elevation of 25°.

Actual firing of the T-34 was accomplished through electrical connection by cable into the tank commander's hatch. Initially, when the rocket launcher system was affixed to the tank turret, the main 75mm gun could not be fired. This issue was addressed by enterprising tank crews in the field by connecting the elevation arm to the gun mantlet to allow the gun to operate at reduced elevation. The launcher assembly weighed 1,840lb and could be jettisoned in the event of close action with or without its rockets in place.

The T-34 was in production prior to D-Day and it was anticipated that the weapon could be used to clear German beach defences along the coast of Normandy. However, by June 6, 1944, this plan had been discarded as the top-heavy tanks were unwieldy for transport by landing craft due to their high centre of gravity. Thus, the T-34s introduction to combat was delayed until later in the year as the US 30th Infantry Division prepared to launch an offensive. These Calliopes, which received their nickname because they looked similar to a pipe organ and screeched as their missiles launched, were received by the 743rd Tank Battalion. After the Battle of the Bulge, larger numbers of T-34s arrived and served into 1945.

Later in World War Two, the M8 was replaced by the M16, which was more accurate, and a modified launcher was introduced. The T-34 saw only limited action to the end of the conflict.

RIGHT: A T-34 Calliope fires its 4.5-inch rockets during combat in France. (US ARMY SIGNAL CORPS VIA WIKIMEDIA COMMONS)

RIGHT: The T40/M17 Whizbang was a 7.2mm rocket launcher that superseded the T-34 and was introduced late in World War Two. (CREATIVE COMMONS GRANING VIA WIKIMEDIA COMMONS)

T-34 Calliope 4.5-inch multiple rocket launcher	
Country of Origin	United States
Calibre	114mm
Crew	4-5
Range	4,200 yards
Rate of Fire	36 rockets in 10 seconds per battery
Number manufactured	225

Nebelwerfer 42 210mm & 300mm

The Screaming Meemie

LEFT: German soldiers moving their 210mm Nebelwerfer 42 into firing position in the field. (CREATIVE COMMONS BUNDESARCHIV BILD VIA WIKIMEDIA COMMONS)

The German military made pioneering strides in the development and deployment of rocket-firing weapons early in World War Two. Among the first of such weapons was the 150mm Nebelwerfer 41, literally translated as 'smoke mortar', which was introduced to the field with the Wehrmacht in 1940, just after the conclusion of the Battle of France. The Nebelwerfer 41 fired fin-stablilised rockets from six tubes atop a two-wheeled carriage and gave way to a pair of larger such weapons, the Nebelwerfer 42 210mm and 300mm, as the war progressed. Collectively the Nebelwerfers were nicknamed by the Allies 'Screaming Meemie' because of their shrill sound upon launching.

The Nebelwerfer 42 rocket launcher was mounted atop the carriages of the 37mm PaK 36 anti-tank gun or the 280mm/320mm launcher carriage. The launcher was a five-barrel weapon that was stabilised with a pivoting

Nebelwerfer 42 210mm and 300mm	
Country of Origin	Germany
Calibre	210mm; 300mm
Crew	4; 6
Range	8,580 yards; 4,980 yards
Rate of Fire	6 rounds in 90 seconds; 6 rounds in 90 seconds
Number manufactured	2,626; 954

missile) rocket, which was nearly four feet long. Firing was completed electrically in a ripple timed for each of its six tubes. Without capability to fire a single rocket at one time, the weapon was vulnerable after each salvo since its signature made it easy to locate for counter battery fire. Quick displacement meant the weapon was out of action for somewhat significant periods on the battlefield in extreme conditions.

The Nebelwerfer 42 210mm and 300mm systems are representative of a family of rocket-firing weapons fielded by the German Army in World War Two.

LEFT: A half-track towing a Nebelwerfer 42 210mm mortar toward the front. (CREATIVE COMMONS BUNDESARCHIV BILD VIA WIKIMEDIA COMMONS)

jack in its firing position. Its 210mm Wurfgranate 42 rocket, manufactured only in high explosive form, was fired with a tremendous report, including a shriek and cloud of flame, smoke, dust and debris. The crew was obliged to seek cover before the weapon was electrically discharged. The system weighed 2,400lb fully loaded and ready to fire, while each barrel was 4ft, 3in long. The 210mm Nebelwerfer 42 appeared in combat for the first time in 1942 and served in North Africa, Italy, France and the Eastern Front. Its rocket ammunition was also adapted for Luftwaffe aircraft.

The 300mm Nebelwerfer followed the 210mm into action in 1943. Its empty weight was 2,400lb and its tubes fired the Wurfkorper 42 Spreng (explosive

BELOW: German troops operate the 300mm Nebelwerfer 42 amid a winter landscape on the Eastern Front in 1944. (CREATIVE COMMONS BUNDESARCHIV BILD VIA WIKIMEDIA COMMONS)

Katyusha

Soviet Little Kate

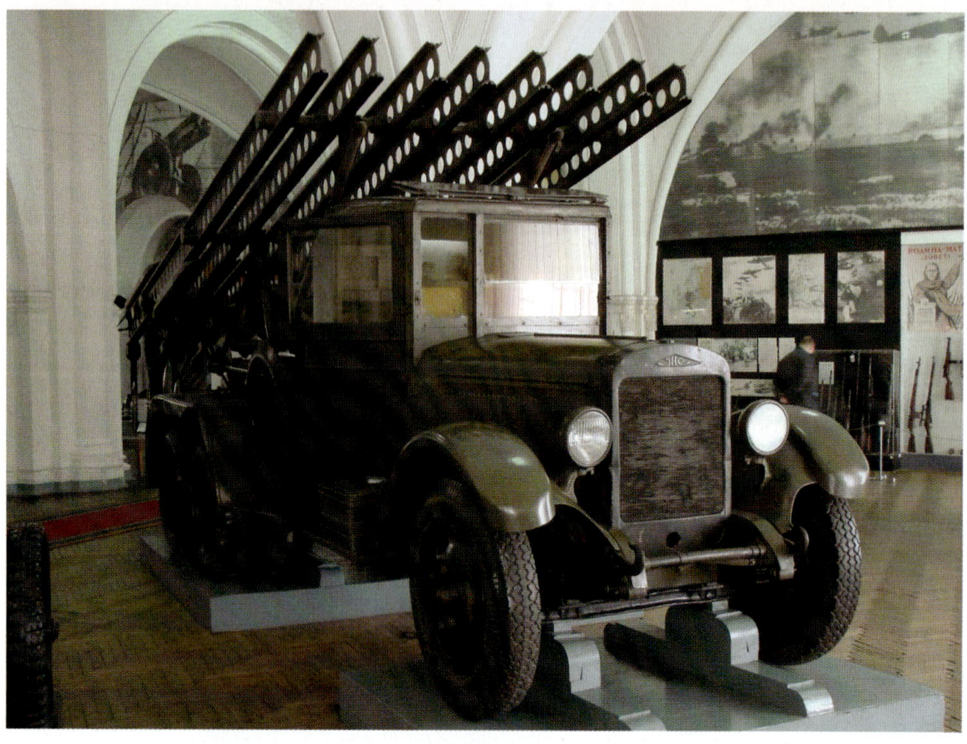

Alongside the T-34 medium tank, the Soviet Red Army's Katyusha rocket launcher is perhaps the most famous Allied weapon to emerge on the Eastern Front during World War Two. Katyusha, literally translated from Russian as 'Little Kate' in reference to a popular wartime song, became a ubiquitous presence on the battlefield, providing heavy firepower and superb mobility for its day.

The most prominent of the Katyusha rocket launcher series to appear during World War Two included the light BM-8, which fired an 82mm rocket, the 132mm rocket firing BM-13 and the heavy BM-31, which launched a 300mm rocket. The mobility and saturation firepower of the Katyusha more than compensated for its lack of accuracy, and the sheer weight of a Katyusha rocket barrage in a confined area wreaked havoc on its intended targets.

The existence of the electrically fired Katyusha was kept secret during much of its development, and it was known by various codenames as the munitions plant at Voronezh was primarily responsible for the most widely used such system during the Great Patriotic War, the BM-13. The Katyusha entered service with the Red Army during the summer of 1941, mounted atop a variety of vehicles for ease of transport and rapid relocation to avoid counter battery fire. These included the ZiS-6 general purpose truck, armoured trains and specifically designed artillery tractors. Variants of the BM-8 were equipped with eight to 48 launch rails that fired the 82mm M8 rocket, while the standard BM-13 mounted 24 rails with variants carrying from six to 16 rails to fire the 132mm M13 rocket that was nearly 32in long. The BM-31 had 12 rails to accommodate the 300mm M-31 rocket, which was 9.7ft long and the system was mounted atop the US-made Studebaker US6 2½-tonne truck.

The simple design assisted in the production of the Katyusha family of rocket launchers. These were fielded on the Eastern Front in batteries that could deliver devastating fire against enemy positions, often with demoralising effect on opposing troops. German soldiers that experienced the firepower of the Katyusha referred to the weapons as 'Stalin's Organs'.

An estimated 10,000 Katyusha rocket launcher systems of all types were produced during World War Two, many of which continued in service with the Red Army or Soviet client states into the 1970s.

Katyusha	
Country of Origin	Soviet Union
Calibre	82mm to 300mm
Crew	6
Range	10,560 yards approximately
Rate of Fire	64 rockets in 10 seconds (battery of 4 BM-13)
Number manufactured	10,000 (post-war estimated total 100,000)

Z Battery & Land Mattress

Bringing the Barrage

British research into rocket weaponry came into its own during the inter-war years and Prime Minister Winston Churchill had become a champion of the effort by the spring of 1940. While serving as First Lord of the Admiralty, Churchill had advocated rocket research to equip ships of the Royal Navy with anti-aircraft rockets capable of bringing down low flying enemy aircraft.

The best known naval rocket weapon was the Z Battery, which became available in the summer of 1940, in time to provide some defence for the home islands during the Battle of Britain. The naval weapon fired a three-inch rocket with a trailing wire and explosive mine at the length, while the land version utilised a high explosive warhead with a specially designed proximity fuse for detonation. Although 7,000 railed rocket projectors were available in August 1940, there was a shortage of rockets and most of these were allocated to the Admiralty and Royal Navy. The initial single rail launcher was designated Projector, 3-inch, Mark I, but this was supplanted by launchers that mounted twin rails and then introduced multiple rails that could unleash barrages of up to 36 rockets.

The first experimental use of the Z Battery occurred in October with a system emplaced at Cardiff, Wales, under the command of Churchill's son-in-law, Major Duncan Sandys. The anti-aircraft Z Batteries were eventually transferred to the Home Guard.

The ground version of the Z Battery was deployed to North Africa with the barrage capable No 4 projector and mounted atop the QF 3-inch 20 cwt anti-aircraft gun trailer. Experience there gave rise to the No 8 projector, which was better known as the Land Mattress.

British and Canadian troops used the Land Mattress late in World War Two, while a similar configuration called the Sea Mattress was introduced for amphibious operations. The Sea Mattress multiple launch rocket system fired five-inch cordite projectiles in salvoes of up to 30 rockets. Mounted on landing craft, the Sea Mattress was intended to saturate enemy positions along invasion beaches. It was utilised during the landings in Italy and on D-Day. The Land Mattress was developed by British Lieutenant Colonel Michael Wardell and, despite somewhat disappointing tests, became operational in 16- or 30-tube launchers mounted atop two-wheeled trailers.

The Land Mattress provided artillery support most notably in the crossings of the Rivers Scheldt and Rhine in the closing months of World War Two.

Land Mattress and Z Battery	
Country of Origin	Great Britain
Calibre	3-inch (76.2mm); 3-inch (76.2mm)
Crew	2; 2 per projector in battery air defence
Range	7,910 yards; 1,500 yards in antiaircraft role
Rate of Fire	4 rockets per second; 20 rockets in .75 seconds
Number manufactured	400; 8,400 by April 1940

BELOW: Home Guard troops load a Z Battery rocket at Merseyside in July 1942. (COLLECTIONS OF THE IMPERIAL WAR MUSEUMS VIA WIKIMEDIA COMMONS)

ABOVE: British soldiers prepare a Land Mattress for firing during the Battle of the Reichswald. (COLLECTIONS OF THE IMPERIAL WAR MUSEUMS VIA WIKIMEDIA COMMONS)

LEFT: A Land Mattress rocket system sits beside a German Nebelwerfer at the Canadian War Museum. (CREATIVE COMMONS MZAJAC VIA WIKIMEDIA COMMONS)

Railway Artillery

Thunder on Rails

The railway gun was the epitome of brute firepower. Massive, intimidating and awesome in stature, it was intended to destroy enemy fortifications and strike fear into the adversary, both military and civilian. However, World War Two proved to be the swan song for these big guns. Although they were conspicuously in service during the conflict, by its end they had been eclipsed by advancing technology.

The railway gun traced its lineage to the 19th Century and, during World War One, the German 211mm Paris Gun was ranged to bombard the French capital city from a remarkable distance of 75 miles. Germany, Great Britain, the United States and Japan all produced railway guns during the inter-war years and these included design elements from earlier weapons. In each case, the railway gun was a ponderous weapon of war.

Railway guns were massive, from the German 800mm *Heavy Gustav* and *Dora* and their 280mm K5, one of which gained enduring fame as *Anzio Annie*, to the British BL 18-inch railway howitzer and 13.5-inch gun and the US coastal defensive weapons that remained in service after World War One. They projected devastating firepower like no other weapon on land, and they combined that strength with mobility. While they were theoretically capable of movement along rail lines, their sheer size often required the installation of specially manufactured track.

In addition, railway guns were often so heavy that they were disassembled for transport, then required huge numbers of soldiers to reassemble and prepare them for combat. At the same time, their size made them conspicuous targets for hostile aircraft. While the K5 was

sometimes hidden in railway tunnels for protection between rounds, the Schwerer Gustav and Dora had no possibility of concealment. A single round from one of these guns weighed an incredible seven tonnes!

With the evolution of technology, including rocket systems, missiles and long-range aircraft, the railway gun became increasingly impractical. The tremendous commitment of resources necessary to maintain them in the field far outweighed their advantages and the expense could be allocated to the manufacture of other weapons.

Today, surviving examples of railway guns may be seen in museums, evidence of a World War Two weapon system that was active and yet simultaneously an anachronism.

Schwerer Gustav

Krupp Steel in Crimea

Although only two examples were ever completed and entered service with the German Wehrmacht, the Schwerer Gustav was the largest calibre rifled weapon ever used in modern warfare and the heaviest mobile artillery piece ever constructed. It was designed at the Krupp facilities in Rügenwalde for specific use against the fortifications of the French Maginot Line.

Development of the Schwerer Gustav began in the late 1930s and it was conceived on a massive scale. The 800mm gun weighed 1,490 tonnes, while its barrel was an incredible 106ft, 8in long. The gun fired armour piercing and high explosive shells that weighed a reported seven tonnes each. The massive weapon was developed at the request of the German Army High Command in 1934 in anticipation of the renewal of conflict with its traditional enemy: France.

Intended to fire a shell capable of penetrating nearly 23ft of hardened concrete, the Schwerer Gustav was designed to do so out of range of any enemy counter battery fire. The gun was built with only elevation capability to 48° in the actual mount, and traverse would be accomplished by movement along a curved track. In addition to its own configuration, specialised tracks, cranes and locomotives were developed to facilitate movement and firing. Although preliminary work was done in succeeding months after the military request, momentum lagged and it was not until 1936 that the effort

Schwerer Gustav	
Country of Origin	Germany
Calibre	800mm
Crew	500
Range	51,000 yards
Rate of Fire	1 round in 30-45 minutes
Number manufactured	2

ABOVE: The 800mm railway gun *Dora* is shown firing at high elevation in June 1942. (BILDENDE KUNST VIA WIKIMEDIA COMMONS)

LEFT: *Dora* on the Eastern Front during the Battle of Stalingrad. (BILDENDE KUNST VIA WIKIMEDIA COMMONS)

was renewed. Some sources state that a visit to Krupp in the city of Essen by the Führer himself jump-started the programme. Blueprints were finished in early 1937 and, in late 1939, the test weapon was finished.

Two guns were eventually ordered. When readied for action, they were mounted atop a specially built railcar with 80 wheels in eight bogies with five axles each. The guns were named *Heavy Gustav* and *Dora* after a senior Krupp official and the wife of the project's chief engineer.

Heavy Gustav was deployed to Crimea in early 1942 and fired in support of German troops at the siege of Sevastopol. Its transport included 25 cars in a train that stretched nearly a mile, and about 250 soldiers were detailed to prepare it for action. Assembly required more than two days of labour. A crew of 500 was responsible for loading, firing and maintenance. *Dora* was moved to the Eastern Front in August 1942 in anticipation of use during the Battle of Stalingrad, but was withdrawn in the face a Red Army offensive.

Both guns were destroyed by German troops in the spring of 1945 to prevent their capture intact by the Allies.

LEFT: This Soviet fortification at Sevastopol was reportedly destroyed by five 800mm shells fired by *Heavy Gustav* in June 1942. (CREATIVE COMMONS BUNDESARCHIV BILD VIA WIKIMEDIA COMMONS)

K5 283mm

Allies meet Anzio Annie

RIGHT: The crew of a K5 283mm railway gun loads a round at the Anzio beachhead in May 1944. (NATIONAL DIGITAL ARCHIVES OF POLAND VIA WIKIMEDIA COMMONS)

For American soldiers in the crucible of the beachhead at Anzio, the sound of incoming shells fired from the hefty German K5 283mm railway gun was unforgettable. The soldiers said it was like a freight train passing, then the concussion shook the earth.

The Germans were foremost in the deployment of railway guns during World War Two. Those that were in action at the embattled toehold north of the Gustav Line in Italy were dubbed *Anzio Annie* or the *Anzio Express*, although the Germans had christened them *Leopold* and *Robert*. The K5 series saw widespread use with German forces in Europe, their 240-tonnes transported atop specially built rail cars. The barrel of the K5 stretched nearly 84ft long.

Like the larger Schwerer Gustav, the K5s were limited in traverse and relied on curved tracks constructed by troops in the field to orient them toward a target that was not in direct line with the forward position of the gun. The weapon fired at a maximum elevation of 50° and its high explosive shells weighed up to 584lb. In time, a rocket-propelled projectile was also introduced. The rocket shell's booster ignited 19 seconds after firing and was said to thrust the warhead into the stratosphere before falling away as descent began to maximum range of 53 miles.

The K5 originated in the mid-1930s under Krupp supervision in the Rügerwalde near the coastline of the Baltic Sea. Design, development and trials led to the production of eight K5 guns before the Nazi invasion of France and the Low Countries in the spring of 1940. Early field action revealed trouble with the rifling of the gigantic barrels, but with structural revisions the K5s were reliable weapons through the end of the conflict.

Despite their heavy firepower and mobility along both civilian and specially built military railroads, the K5s were also dependent on substantial manpower for transport and establishment in firing position. They were mobile enough to find cover in railroad tunnels between rounds, but remained susceptible to air attack while in the open. As technology advanced and Allied air power gained control over the skies of Europe, the K5 became more and more vulnerable.

The *Leopold* and *Robert* guns were captured by American troops in Italy shortly after the liberation of Rome. *Robert* had been severely damaged by retreating German troops, but *Leopold* survived, underwent repairs and was shipped to the US for evaluation and preservation as a museum piece. Another K5 gun is on display in France.

RIGHT: German crewmembers clean the barrel of a K5 railway gun just outside a tunnel along an Italian rail line. (CREATIVE COMMONS BUNDESARCHIV BILD VIA WIKIMEDIA COMMONS)

BELOW: K5 283mm railway gun at Civitavecchia, Italy on June 9, 1944. (US NAVAL HISTORY AND HERITAGE COMMAND PHOTO VIA WIKIMEDIA COMMONS)

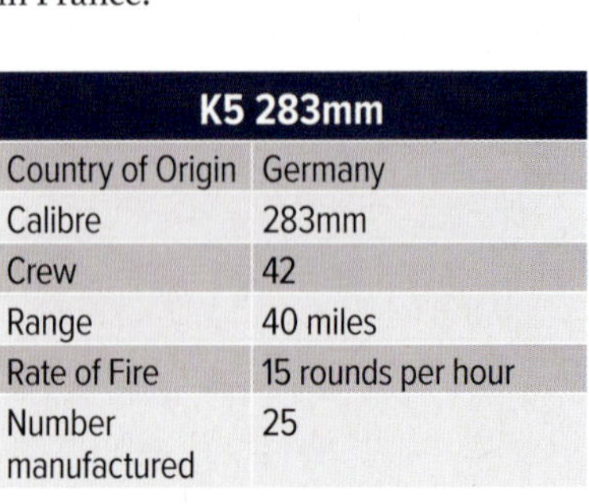

K5 283mm	
Country of Origin	Germany
Calibre	283mm
Crew	42
Range	40 miles
Rate of Fire	15 rounds per hour
Number manufactured	25

K12E 210mm

Throughout World War Two, Germany were determined to bring the conflict to the British Isles. From the Battle of Britain to the contemplation of Operation Sea Lion, an actual invasion of Britain, they sought to undermine the morale of the British people in the process.

One lesser known undertaking was the development of the K12E 210mm railway gun.

The K12E weighed 333 tonnes and its barrel was 109ft, 3in long, which required external support to prevent the barrel from bending or sagging under its own weight. The gun operated with a horizontal sliding block breech, and its range was sufficient to fire a projectile to a maximum distance of 71 miles and, under normal conditions, an effective range of 28 miles. From emplacements on the coast of France, the K12E was capable of shelling areas across the English Channel and into England itself. S – shell fragments were once discovered in Kent, 55 miles from the closest point in France. In action, the barrel support caused the breech to be quite close to the ground. To correct this hazardous situation, a hydraulic jack was installed to raise the breech between rounds. Modifications were made later with the introduction of balancing presses to address the issue.

The inspiration for the K12E was derived from the Paris Gun of World War One, which shelled the French capital from a distance of 75 miles. Krupp engineers had maintained their interest in the production of heavy railway guns during the inter-war years, with the K12E being tested in the mid-1930s, with the first operational gun completed in 1938 and reaching service with the Wehrmacht the following year. Built on a specially designed carriage of steel beams, two frames were then attached to railroad wheels in a double bogey configuration. During transport, the gun's barrel was disconnected from the hydropneumatic recoil system and receded nearly five feet to reduce the length of the entire weapon.

Two examples of the K12E were completed by 1940 and both were assigned to a German coastal defence battery for the duration of the war.

K12E 210mm	
Country of Origin	Germany
Calibre	210mm
Crew	40
Range	28 miles (effective)
Rate of Fire	6 rounds per hour
Number manufactured	2

BELOW: The crew of a K12E 210mm watch an artist at work along the French coastline with their weapon in the background. (CREATIVE COMMONS BUNDESARCHIV BILD VIA WIKIMEDIA COMMONS)

ABOVE: German officers watch the loading of a tank for Operation Sea Lion, which never took place. The K12E might have fired in support had the Germans landed in Britain. (CREATIVE COMMONS BUNDESARCHIV BILD VIA WIKIMEDIA COMMONS)

LEFT: A 210mm K12E railway gun prepares to fire from a position along the coast of the English Channel in France. (ZWEITEN WELTKRIEG VIA WIKIMEDIA COMMONS)

BL 9.2-inch Mk XIII

Great War to Home Defence

Courtesy of the Royal Navy surplus, the 9.2-inch gun did not disappear from British service when it was replaced in warship armament. In fact, early examples and improved descendants of the 9.2-inch gun remained active for the next half-century.

During World War Two, the BL 9.2-inch Mk XIII railway gun was a stalwart component of the home defence against potential Nazi invasion. It was positioned along likely landing beaches on the southern and eastern coasts of Britain and intended to repel not only enemy forces at their insertion point, but also bombard any areas temporarily occupied, such as troop marshalling centres or airfields. Although its firing of practice rounds caused some damage to homes in nearby populated areas, it was generally comforting to see the big gun in position. Sensitive to disruption, authorities later attempted to place the Mk XIII in rural areas as much as possible.

With its railway origin stretching back to the Second Boer War, in which it was deployed at Belfast, northeast of Johannesburg, but never fired, the 9.2-inch railway gun was adapted at the works of the Elswick Ordnance Company in 1915 at the height of World War One. Mounted on railway carriages for use on the Western Front in France,

RIGHT: Crewmen stand by their camouflaged 9.2-inch railway gun ready to fire in fading daylight. (COLLECTIONS OF THE IMPERIAL WAR MUSEUMS VIA WIKIMEDIA COMMONS)

BL 9.2-inch Mk XIII	
Country of Origin	Great Britain
Calibre	9.2-inch (233.7mm)
Crew	14
Range	22,600 yards
Rate of Fire	2 rounds per minute
Number manufactured	Unknown

BELOW: This BL 9.2-inch Mk XIII railway gun is pictured atop its riveted rail carriage. (PUBLIC DOMAIN UNKNOWN AUTHOR VIA WIKIMEDIA COMMONS)

they provided heavy fire support to British infantry. The guns were fitted with an interrupted screw breech and recoiled on slides. Their traverse was up to 10° left or right, with modifications that raised elevation to 35°.

By 1939, the purpose-built Mk XIII gun had been in service since World War One. Its heavier breech, elevation to 40° and longer range at 22,600 yards appeared to validate the investment in the new construction rather than a continuation of the surplus naval guns that preceded it. The heavier breech brought the trunnions in closer, shortening the depression of the breech as the gun was elevated. When brought to firing position along its rail line, the Mk XIII was stabilised by outriggers and later by the laying of rail spurs that included ground anchors for better recoil absorption.

The Mk XIII fired a high explosive shell that weighed 380lb. Its barrel length was 35ft, 10in, and it weighed more than 27 tonnes.

BL 18-inch Howitzer & 13.5-inch Gun

Repurposed for Railway Service

The BL 18-inch railway howitzer was characteristic of the introduction of heavier weapons onto the battlefields of World War One, but its development was too slow to see action. It did not become available for service until 1920.

After World War One, such weapons were not deemed practical due to their short range and logistical burden, although the big howitzer was tested at Shoeburyness, Essex, before being stored for 20 years, probably at the Royal Arsenal in Woolwich. However, with the outbreak of World War Two, a single BL 18-inch howitzer was taken from storage and mounted on a rail carriage nickname *Boche Buster* that had carried a 14-inch gun during World War One.

One of three heavy railway guns deployed in 1940, the 18-inch howitzer was transported on the Elham Valley Railway line across Kent and stationed at Bourne Park. Although its range was insufficient to fire at German positions across the English Channel, it was considered a formidable weapon in the event the Wehrmacht attempted to land in Britain. It weighed nearly 88 tonnes, while its barrel was 52ft long and fired a 2,500-pound high explosive shell. A single barrel survives today at the Royal Armouries artillery museum at Fort Nelson, Hampshire.

The BL 13.5-inch Mk V naval gun was a veteran of the epic 1916 Battle of Jutland that found extended service life in conversion to a railway gun. In 1939, three World War One-era BL 14-inch railway guns were removed from storage at the Royal Army Ordnance Corps Chilwell depot and placed in service. The barrels of the original 14-inch guns had long been sold as scrap, so the available 13.5-inch Mk Vs that had been salvaged from the Royal Navy Iron Duke-class super dreadnought battleships were modified as rail guns during the next year and entered service with the Royal Marine Siege Regiment at Dover.

The first of the guns was nicknamed *HMG (His Majesty's Gun) Scene-Shifter*, which entered service in November 1940. *Scene-Shifter* was followed by *HMG Piece-Maker* and *HMG Gladiator*. Their range was sufficient to reach the Pas de Calais in Nazi-occupied France, and occasionally a round was loosed in that direction. Preliminary plans for their deployment to France as artillery support weapons after D-Day were never realised.

The BL 13.5-inch railway gun weighed 84 tonnes, and its barrel stretched just over 52ft and it fired a high explosive shell that weighed 1,250lb.

ABOVE: The BL 13.5-inch Mk V in turret aboard the battleship HMS *Ajax* in 1912. (GOVERNMENT OF THE UNITED KINGDOM VIA WIKIMEDIA COMMONS)

LEFT: The BL 18-inch with British officers at Halwill Junction during World War Two. (GOVERNMENT OF THE UNITED KINGDOM VIA WIKIMEDIA COMMONS)

BL 18-inch Railway Howitzer & 13.5-inch Railway Gun	
Country of Origin	Great Britain
Calibre	18-inch (457mm); 13.5-inch (343mm)
Crew	24; 47
Range	22,300 yards; 40,000 yards
Rate of Fire	1 round per 2 minutes; 1 round per 2 minutes
Number manufactured	5; 206

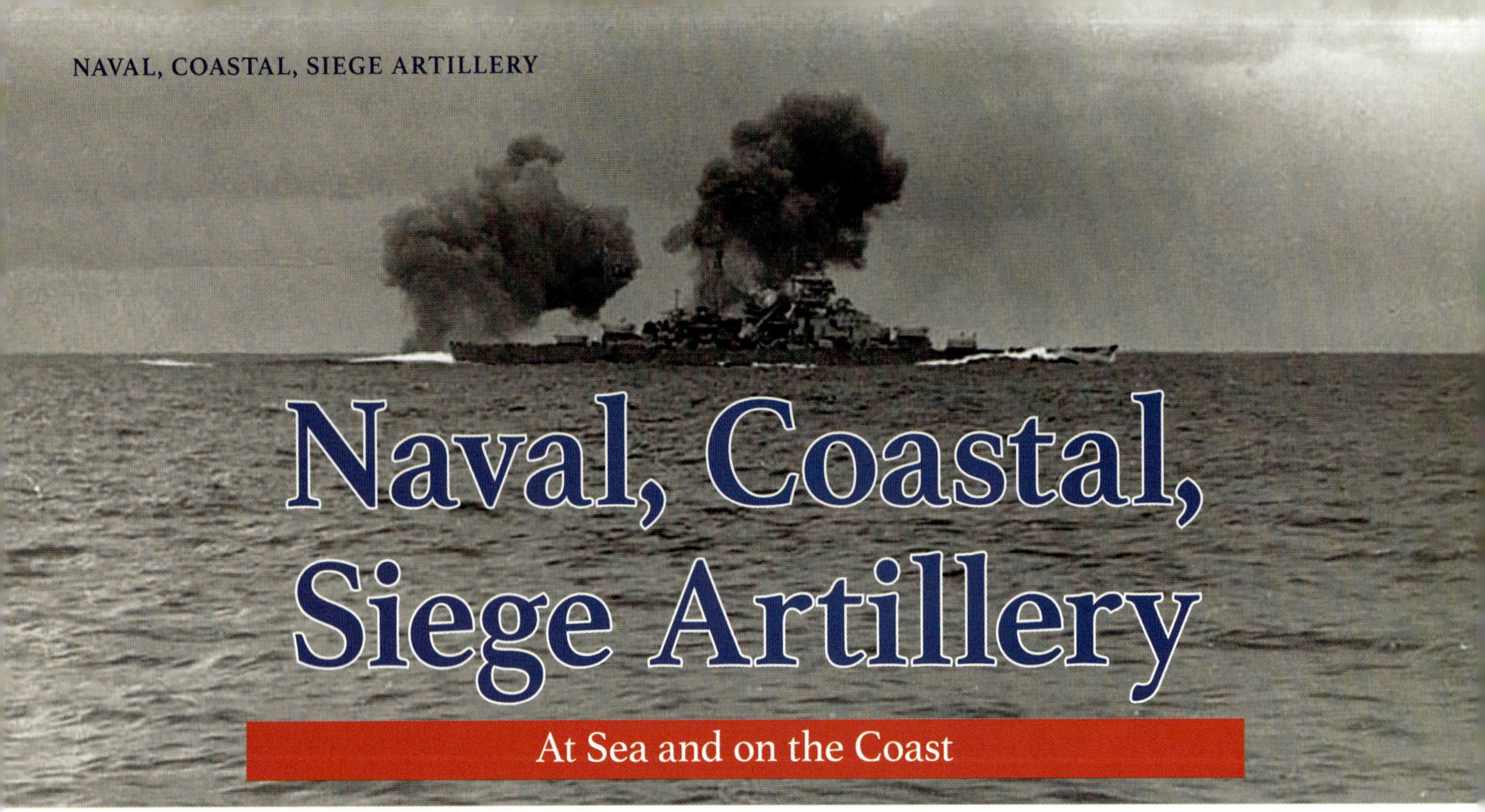

Naval, Coastal, Siege Artillery

At Sea and on the Coast

ABOVE: The German battleship *Bismarck* firing its main 15-inch batteries at HMS *Hood* during the Battle of the Denmark Strait, May 1941. (CREATIVE COMMONS BUNDESARCHIV BILD VIA WIKIMEDIA COMMONS)

They were the big guns that defined World War Two at sea, defended coastlines and pounded besieged cities into rubble. These weapons were already in their twilight due to advancing technology that traded missiles for massive shells, aircraft to dominate the oceans rather than the dreadnought and nuclear weapons for unprecedented devastation rather than the prolonged agony of a fight that might seem to never end. It marked the end of battles between capital ships exchanging broadsides to decide the fate of empires, a standard of conflict that stretched back to the age of sail.

The world's great navies sent their battleships to sea during the conflict. Their heavy weapons fired at defences ashore, sometimes softening up embattled ground for amphibious landings, raiding commerce and merchant vessels and ranging against one another.

It was the big 15-inch guns of *Bismarck* that sent the legendary battlecruiser HMS *Hood* to its tragic end in the Denmark Strait and then the thunder of *King George V* and *Rodney* that exacted retribution. The 14-inch main batteries of HMS *Duke of York* sank the German battlecruiser *Scharnhorst* in the 1943 Battle of the North Cape. The 14- and 16-inch naval rifles of US Navy battleships, raised from the mud of Pearl Harbor, fired with vengeance at Surigao Strait and blasted the Japanese task force. The Imperial Japanese Navy sent *Yamato* with 18-inch main batteries to wreak havoc off Samar and it later sank under a hail of bombs and torpedoes.

The coastal guns provided the bark that backed concrete and steel defences, occasionally lobbing shells at distant enemy positions or deterring aggression just by their mere presence. They worried invasion planners and gave the Allies pause in the run-up to D-Day, so much so that countless bomber sorties pummelled the casemates and fortifications of the Atlantic Wall and a handful of American Rangers scaled the cliffs at Pointe du Hoc to seek and destroy a menacing battery.

Heavy siege cannon had proven their worth in past conflicts, most recently in the Russo-Japanese War, when the Japanese unleashed 280mm Krupp-built howitzers to pound the Russian defences of Port Arthur. Siege guns were employed on occasion across the globe during World War Two, but as fearsome as they might be, their days were numbered. For the types of artillery seen in these pages, their strength is apparent, but their last days of widespread military relevance were at hand in the mid-20th Century.

RIGHT: Salvaged after being sunk at Pearl Harbor, the battleship USS *West Virginia* is shown in 1944, her eight 16-inch main guns visible. (US NAVAL HISTORY AND HERITAGE COMMAND VIA WIKIMEDIA COMMONS)

RIGHT: The barrel of a German coastal defence gun of the Atlantic Wall in France. (CREATIVE COMMONS BUNDESARCHIV BILD VIA WIKIMEDIA COMMONS)

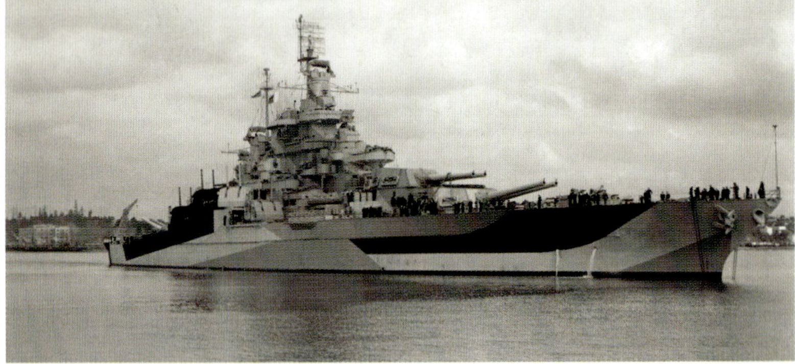

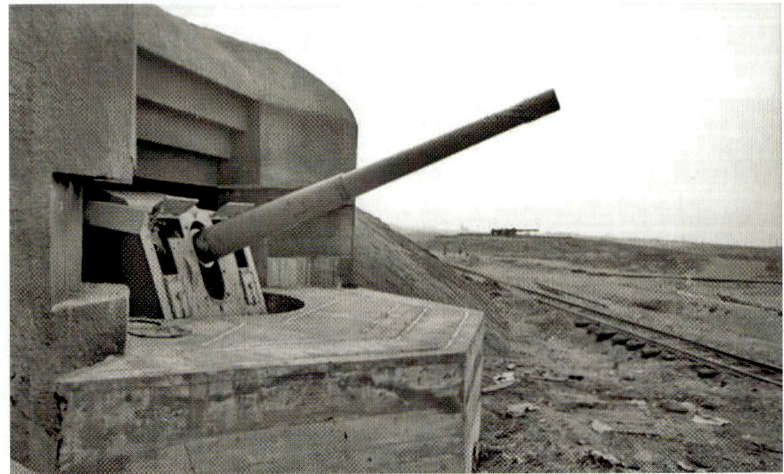

14-inch 45 & 50-calibre

U.S. Navy Main Battery

The powerful punch of US Navy battleships constructed in the early years of the 20th Century included two types of 14-inch main weaponry: the 45- and 50-calibre guns.

The 45-calibre gun was upgraded through the 1930s and employed in several variants or marks. As the first such heavy guns to be adopted by the US Navy, they constituted the main batteries of the New York-, Nevada- and Pennsylvania-class battleships. The origin of the 14-inch 45-calibre gun dated to 1910 with a design by the Bureau of Ordnance and production was undertaken by the US Naval Gun Factory at the Washington Navy Yard, Bethlehem Steel and the Midvale Steel Company. The gun was in service during World War One and aboard several battleships whose service lives extended into World War Two.

Later marks included upgrades to increase propellant charges and muzzle velocity to extend the range of the guns, and the battleships armed with the 45-calibre weapons participated in numerous operations in the Atlantic and Pacific. *Texas* and *New York* bombarded the coast of North Africa during Operation Torch in November 1942, while

14-inch 45 and 50-calibre	
Country of Origin	United States
Calibre	14-inch (356mm); 14-inch (356mm)
Crew	67; 98
Range	23,000 yards; 36,800 yards
Rate of Fire	1.75 rounds per minute; 2 rounds per minute
Number manufactured	78; 119

Texas and *Nevada* supported the D-Day landings on June 6, 1944, and duelled with German shore batteries. *Pennsylvania* participated in the Aleutian campaign against the Japanese occupiers of the islands of Attu and Kiska. *Oklahoma* and *Arizona* were destroyed at Pearl Harbor on December 7, 1941. The British Royal Navy adopted the 14-inch 45-calibre gun as the BL 14-inch Mk II, which saw service during World War One. The Mark I 14-inch 45-calibre gun weighed more than 142,000lb with a barrel length of nearly 53ft and fired a 1,400-pound armour piercing shell up to 23,000 yards.

The 14-inch 50-calibre naval gun was designed in 1916 as the main armament of the planned Lexington-class battlecruiser. When these warship designs were abandoned with the Washington Naval Treaty of 1922, the guns were transferred to the New Mexico-class battleships and entered service in 1918. The gun was produced in four variants and its barrel was more than 58ft long. The gun fired various types of armour piercing shells of 1,275 to 1,500 pounds to a maximum range of 36,800 yards, a significant increase over the 45-calibre version. Along with the New Mexico-class ships, the 50-calibre gun was installed aboard the battleships *Mississippi*, *Idaho*, *Tennessee* and *California*.

During World War Two, *Tennessee* – lead ship of its own class – *Mississippi* and *California* were present at Surigao Strait after modernisation and participated in shore bombardment operations across the Pacific. All five battleships were in service through to the end of the conflict.

ABOVE: The 14-inch 45-calibre guns of the battleship USS *Nevada* fire at targets on Utah Beach on D-Day. (US NAVY VIA WIKIMEDIA COMMONS)

LEFT: A 14-inch 45-calibre aboard a Royal Navy Abercrombie-class monitor. (GOVERNMENT OF THE UNITED KINGDOM VIA WIKIMEDIA COMMONS)

LEFT: The main 14-inch 50-calibre guns of the battleship USS *Tennessee* fire in support of the landings on Okinawa on April 1, 1945. (NAVAL HISTORY AND HERITAGE COMMAND VIA WIKIMEDIA COMMONS)

16-inch 45 & 50-calibre

Heavy Duty on the Ocean

ABOVE: The battleship USS *Iowa* fires a broadside with its 16-inch 50-calibre Mark.7 main batteries. (US NAVY VIA WIKIMEDIA COMMONS)

RIGHT: These 16-inch 45-calibre Mark 6 guns are shown aboard the battleship USS *South Dakota* in 1943. (US NAVY VIA WIKIMEDIA COMMONS)

As the era of the big-gun battleship reached its zenith in World War Two, the limitations of the Washington and London Naval Treaties impacted the size and firepower of their main batteries. The US Navy employed 16-inch main battery guns during the war years that were intended to both improve performance with numerous upgrades while also maintaining early compliance with treaty restrictions.

The 16-inch 45-calibre Mark 1 gun was tested in 1914 and approved for production three years later at the Watervliet Arsenal and Bethlehem Steel. These guns were constructed for the Colorado-class battleships with a barrel length of 60ft and maximum firing range of 35,000 yards. In the 1930s, upgrades were made with the Mark 5 and Mark 8 to include a larger chamber to allow heavier propellant charges and chromium plated bore for longer barrel life.

The North Carolina-class battleships were constructed under treaty restrictions and the Mark 6 14-inch 45-calibre gun improved on the Mark 1 with a lighter three-barrel turret, while firing a 2,240-pound shell to a range of 35,000 yards. Later improvements allowed the gun to fire a potent 2,700-pound armour piercing shell as well. The Mark 6 rendered significant service during World War Two with USS *Massachusetts* firing at targets in Casablanca, including the Vichy French battleship *Jean Bart* during Operation Torch, the Allied invasion of North Africa. The USS *Washington* targeted the Japanese battleship *Kirishima* at the Naval Battle of Guadalcanal in November 1942, inflicting fatal damage.

The 16-inch 50-calibre Mark 7 was perhaps the finest naval gun ever developed for a battleship. It constituted the main batteries of the legendary Iowa-class battleships and was introduced to service in 1943, four years after development was undertaken. The Mark 7 was a lightweight turreted weapon compared to earlier types, with barrels stretching nearly 67ft and weight of 267,900lb. The Mark 7 was built with a chromium plate bore that extended barrel life and was paired with the Ford Instrument Company Mark 8 Range Keeper, an early computer that worked in combination with advanced radar target acquisition to allow accurate fire at maximum range in daytime or nocturnal engagements. Each gun barrel could be elevated independently to a maximum of 45°.

The Iowa-class battleships included the lead ship, *Missouri*, *Wisconsin* and *New Jersey*. Intermittently retired and then reactivated, *Wisconsin* and *Iowa* served into the 1990s.

RIGHT: The 16-inch 45-calibre guns of the battleship USS *Massachusetts* shelling the Japanese home island of Honshu. (US NAVY VIA WIKIMEDIA COMMONS)

16-inch 45 & 50-calibre	
Country of Origin	United States
Calibre	16-inch (406mm)
Crew	180; 79
Range	36,953 yards; 42,240 yards
Rate of Fire	2 rounds per minute; 2 rounds per minute
Number manufactured	28; 36

5-inch 38-calibre Mark 12

Versatile and Powerful Destroyer Weapon

LEFT: These 5-inch 38-calibre guns are shown in single mounts aboard a US Navy destroyer. (US NAVY VIA WIKIMEDIA COMMONS)

5-Inch 38-Calibre Mark 12	
Country of Origin	United States
Calibre	5-inch (127mm)
Crew	15-27
Range	18,000 yards or 37,200 feet altitude
Rate of Fire	12-22 rounds per minute
Number manufactured	8,000 minimum

LEFT: A gun crew demonstrates the loading procedure with a 5-inch 38-calibre gun in open pedestal mount. (US NAVY VIA WIKIMEDIA COMMONS)

fire. Initial issues with deployment were overcome to deliver one of the most reliable weapons of World War Two. Paired with the modern Mark 37 Fire Control System, the gun was highly accurate in day or night action. It was installed on virtually every major warship built for the US Navy from 1939 to 1946. The British Royal Navy operated the weapon when it was installed aboard the destroyer HMS *Delhi* during refitting at the New York Navy Yard, but demand for the gun aboard US vessels prevented a wider distribution with the Royal Navy.

The 5-inch 38-calibre gun remained in service after World War Two aboard warships sold to other nations. It was active on US Navy warships for decades and further retained in the reserve fleet.

BELOW: The 5-inch 38-calibre Mark 12 gun in dual mounts aboard the destroyer USS *Porter*. (US NAVY VIA WIKIMEDIA COMMONS)

Considered by many observers and ordnance experts to be the finest dual-purpose naval gun of World War Two, the 5-Inch 38-Calibre Mark12 was adept in the anti-surface role against enemy warships and shore targets, as well as in anti-aircraft defence, with its sustained rate of fire effective against planes that were generally shot down by shell fragments rather than direct hits.

Design work to replace the earlier 5-inch 25-calibre gun began in the early 1930s and the 5-inch 38-calibre weapon entered service aboard the destroyer USS *Farragut* in 1934. Original pedestal mounts were later replaced with base ring mounting that incorporated shell hoists, with shells and propellant cartridges transported directly to the gun breech for greater efficiency. This upgrade was introduced with the destroyer USS *Porter* in 1936.

The gun weighed 3,990lb and with the mount the total weight varied widely to more than 170,000lb. The barrel stretched nearly 19ft and the gun was placed in both single and dual mounts, becoming the main armament on standard destroyers and secondary armament among larger warships built into the 1940s. Many World War One-vintage ships that remained in service were refitted with the 5-inch 38-calibre gun.

Although the weapon was loaded by hand, its power-ramming equipment delivered a high rate of

8-inch 55-calibre Mark 12 & 15

Standard Heavy Cruiser Main Battery

8-Inch 55-Calibre Mark 12 & Mark 15	
Country of Origin	United States
Calibre	8-inch (203mm)
Crew	44
Range	30,050 yards
Rate of Fire	3 rounds per minute
Number manufactured	Unknown

RIGHT: Officers pose in front of a forward 8-inch 55-calibre gun aboard the heavy cruiser USS *Indianapolis*. (NATIONAL MUSEUM OF THE U.S. NAVY VIA WIKIMEDIA COMMONS)

The main battery weapons of several US Navy heavy cruiser classes of the World War Two era, the 8-inch 55-Calibre Mark 12 and Mark 15 guns were indicative of a series whose service spanned half-a-century, stretching into the 1970s.

US Navy designers began work on the 8-inch gun in 1933 to provide a lighter weapon than its predecessor, the 8-inch 55-calibre Mark 9, in order to comply with the terms of the Washington Naval Treaty. Reducing the gun's weight from 30 tonnes to 17 tonnes, the new Mark 12 was constructed with forgings from Bethlehem Steel and Midvale Steel, assembled at the Naval Gun Factory in the Washington Navy Yard and further manufactured at the Watervliet Arsenal before completion.

The weight reduction was accomplished largely by the elimination of hoops or the shrinking of multiple barrel layers together, while utilising a chromium-lined barrel to increase longevity. Two gun mountings, twin and triple, were developed. The gun incorporated a down-swinging Welin breech block, while each was individually sleeved and mounted further apart in the turret to achieve better shell accuracy and dispersion. The barrel extended nearly 37ft, and the gun fired a 260-pound high explosive or 335-pound armour piercing projectile. The Mark 12 was introduced in 1939 and mounted aboard the aircraft carriers *Lexington* and *Saratoga* until they were removed in 1942. The Mark 15 was quite similar to the Mark 12, but included a reshaped chamber and rifling similar to that of the Mark 14, third in the series of five 8-inch 55-calibre guns produced.

The Mark 12 and Mark 15 became standard on the US Navy's Tuscaloosa sub-class (similar to the New Orleans-class), Wichita-class and Baltimore-class, while the Mark 15 was mounted on some of the Baltimore-class warships and four Oregon City-class heavy cruisers. The Mark 12 and Mark 15 remained in service through the Korean and Vietnam wars and were replaced in the 1970s, initially by the Mark 71 8-inch 55-calibre gun and then the Mark 45.

BELOW LEFT: An 8-inch 55-calibre gun mount damaged after the USS *New Orleans* was struck by a Japanese torpedo at the Battle of Tassafaronga in November 1942. (US NAVY VIA WIKIMEDIA COMMONS)

BELOW RIGHT: The heavy cruiser USS *Helena* fires its Mark 15 8-inch 55-calibre guns during the Korean War. (US NAVY VIA WIKIMEDIA COMMONS)

6-inch 47-calibre Mark 16

The 6-Inch 47-calibre Mark 16 naval gun constituted the main armament of many of the US Navy's World War Two light cruisers, including the Brooklyn and Cleveland classes. The Cleveland-class warships were the most numerous of their type ever built, and the designation 'Mark 16' indicated that the gun was the 16th of its kind produced for the US Navy.

Naval designers developed the gun in response to shortcomings of the preceding 6-inch 152mm Mark 8 and to remain in compliance with the Washington Naval Treaty. Its firepower was stepped up to utilise armour piercing ammunition labelled 'super heavy', with penetrating capability that doubled earlier weapons. The Mark 16 barrel extended 23½ft and the armour piercing projectile weighed 130lb. The gun was typically installed in a triple turret and was intended for use against surface targets, although an anti-aircraft variant, the Mark 16DP, was installed in a twin turret in a dual-purpose role that was evaluated beginning in 1940. The Mark 17 derivative was designed to use bagged propellant, but was installed on only one gunboat on a single pedestal mount.

Individual Mark 16 guns weighed 6.5 tonnes, while a triple turret weighed up to 167 tonnes. The weapon was semiautomatic and utilised a vertical sliding breech bloc, and its disposition in triple turrets along the centerline of the light cruiser allowed the firing of full broadsides, unlike the preceding Omaha-class light cruisers that were restricted to eight-gun broadsides due to emplacement in single casemates, although they also carried 12 6-inch guns.

During trials off Guantanamo Bay in Cuba in the spring of 1939, the light cruiser USS *Savannah* achieved an exceptionally high rate of fire and the warship captain reported that his target was "simply smothered." The cruiser *Honolulu*'s captain reported: "Those who saw this practice said it looked almost like a stream of bullets playing on the targets, which were almost continuously obscured and drenched by water."

As the exercise proceeded, gunners aboard *Savannah* improved their accuracy, firing 14 shells well short of the target followed by 14 that fell beyond, then full rapid fire that unleashed 138 shells in one minute.

6-Inch 47-Calibre Mark 16	
Country of Origin	United States
Calibre	6-inch (152mm)
Crew	55
Range	26,118 yards
Rate of Fire	8-10 rounds per minute
Number manufactured	216

LEFT: The light cruiser USS *Phoenix* fires its 6-inch guns during the Battle of Leyte Gulf, October 1944. (NATIONAL MUSEUM OF THE U.S. NAVY VIA WIKIMEDIA COMMONS)

LEFT: A 6-inch 47-calibre gun mount aboard the cruiser USS *Boise* shows the effect of a hit from a Japanese shell. (US NAVY VIA WIKIMEDIA COMMONS)

BELOW: The 6-inch batteries of the light cruiser USS *Brooklyn* with spent shell casings strewn about the deck during Operation Husky in Sicily in July 1943. (US NAVY VIA WIKIMEDIA COMMONS)

M1919 16-inch 50-calibre Coastal Defence Gun

Protecting the North American Continent

Coastal defence – protecting the major cities and harbours of the country – was a major responsibility of the US Army during the 19th and early 20th Centuries. Fortifications were constructed and large coastal artillery emplacements and casemates were built to house heavy guns with the ability to engage hostile warships at a distance.

The US Army Coast Artillery Corps is known to have positioned its first 16-inch gun at Fort Grant in the Panama Canal Zone to defend its Pacific side. This gun was in position from 1914 to 1943 and traced its origin to the Watervliet Arsenal in 1895. The second type of 16-inch coastal defence gun, the M1919, came into the possession of the army largely through the evolution of US Navy shipbuilding programmes that were required to comply with treaty obligations and rendered some weaponry unusable aboard capital ships.

With the cancellation of the Lexington-class battlecruisers in the 1920s, the main 16-inch 50 calibre guns intended for them became surplus. The second 16-inch guns were built in a similar way to the 1895 model from the

Watervliet Arsenal and were primarily constructed at the Washington Navy Yard. A single gun weighed 484 tonnes while its barrel stretched 66ft, eight in and its armour piercing shell weighed up to 2,340lb. The guns were mounted in disappearing carriages as well as twin barbettes. They were manufactured by a process known as the 'wire wound method', which was common in Europe but rarely used in the United States.

After the big guns were standardised by the Army Coast Artillery, they were deployed in the 1920s to protect major American cities such as New York and Boston, along with Pearl Harbor in Hawaii and locations in Massachusetts, Rhode Island, California and elsewhere. The guns were capable of an elevation of 65° to provide plunging fire to enhance

penetration capabilities against approaching enemy warships.

The probability of direct enemy attack against the US coast had diminished substantially by 1943 and the deployment of further M1919 guns was suspended. In time, the concept of coastal defence was rendered obsolete and most of the guns were scrapped after World War Two.

M1919 16-inch 50-calibre Coastal Defence Gun	
Country of Origin	United States
Calibre	16-inch (406mm)
Crew	30
Range	49,100 yards
Rate of Fire	2 rounds per minute
Number manufactured	50+

BL 14-inch Mk VII

Royal Navy Battleship Punch

The BL 14-inch Mk VII naval gun gained lasting fame during World War Two. It was the primary weapon of the battleships HMS *King George V* and HMS *Prince of Wales* during the epic 1941 chase and sinking of the Nazi battleship *Bismarck*, as well as the main armament of the battleship HMS *Duke of York* during the 1943 Battle of the North Cape which saw the sinking of the Kriegsmarine battlecruiser *Scharnhorst*.

The design of the BL 14-inch Mk VII was undertaken in 1937 to maintain compliance with the terms of the Washington and London Naval Treaties, and modifications to turret configuration from three four-gun installations to two four-gun and one two-gun turret were made. The change allowed more tonnage to be devoted to armour protection and facilitated turret operation as well. The second contributing factor in the development of the new gun was the disappointing performance of the high-velocity 16-inch 45-calibre gun fitted to Nelson-class battleships.

Opting for a lower velocity gun did indeed make those battleships the most lightly armed warships of the period. The BL 14-inch gun was based on the earlier 12-inch 50-calibre Mk XIV from 1933 and entered service with the Royal Navy in 1940. It was built with a radial expansion construction process rather than the earlier wire wound method, which led to a lighter and stronger weapon that was not as susceptible to fatigue and curvature of the barrel. The gun weighed up to approximately 80 tonnes, its barrel stretched 52ft, 6in, and it was constructed at the Royal Gun Factory, Beardmore, Vickers-Armstrong and Elswick Ordnance Company.

Early mechanical difficulties with the turrets were experienced in combat by HMS *Prince of Wales* during the Battle of the Denmark Strait and

by *King George V* in the final action with *Bismarck*, but many of these had been corrected by 1943. *Duke of York* put on a strong showing of firepower and accuracy during the Battle of the North Cape, dispatching *Scharnhorst* with an estimated 52 straddles of the enemy warship in approximately 80 broadsides.

In a historical footnote, the BL 14-inch 50-calibre gun was used as a coastal defence weapon. Two of them, nicknamed *Winnie* and *Pooh*, were mounted in Dover to fire on German guns in Nazi-occupied France.

TOP: The battleship HMS *Duke of York* firing a full broadside from its 14-inch 50-calibre guns during a 1942 exercise. (COLLECTIONS OF THE IMPERIAL WAR MUSEUMS VIA WIKIMEDIA COMMONS)

ABOVE: Winston Churchill aboard HMS *Prince of Wales* with its 14-inch 50-calibre guns en route to meet US President Franklin Roosevelt in 1941. (COLLECTIONS OF THE IMPERIAL WAR MUSEUMS VIA WIKIMEDIA COMMONS)

LEFT: Crewmen aboard the battleship HMS *Duke of York* with a 14-inch 50-calibre gun at Scapa Flow after the 1943 Battle of the North Cape. (COLLECTIONS OF THE IMPERIAL WAR MUSEUMS VIA WIKIMEDIA COMMONS)

BL 14-inch 50-calibre Mk VII	
Country of Origin	Great Britain
Calibre	14-inch (356mm)
Crew	98
Range	38,600 yards
Rate of Fire	2 rounds per minute
Number manufactured	78

BL 15-inch & 16-inch Mk I

RIGHT: A Queen Elizabeth-class battleship fires its BL 15-inch Mk I guns during exercises in 1939. (STATE LIBRARY OF VICTORIA VIA WIKIMEDIA COMMONS)

RIGHT: The forward BL 15-inch Mk I guns of the battlecruiser HMS *Renown* in Mk I (N) mounts are shown in this 1945 image. (COLLECTIONS OF THE IMPERIAL WAR MUSEUMS VIA WIKIMEDIA COMMONS)

BELOW: The BL 16-inch Mk I triple turreted guns are prominent aboard the battleship HMS *Rodney*. (COLLECTIONS OF THE IMPERIAL WAR MUSEUMS VIA WIKIMEDIA COMMONS)

Designed by Vickers, Son and Maxim (acquired by Vickers in 1896) in 1912, the BL 15-inch Mk I was the most common heavy weapon of the Royal Navy for decades. It was installed on battleships and other capital ships for 44 years, from 1915 through 1959, and was originally intended for the Queen Elizabeth-class battleships that were built in response to German naval construction during the arms race that occurred in the years prior to World War One.

The BL 15-inch Mk I was also the main weapon of the five Revenge-class battleships, the Renown-class battlecruisers and several other types. The last to mount the gun was the single battleship of the Vanguard-class completed in 1946. Many naval historians have deemed the gun the most successful of its type in British naval history.

The type was developed rapidly given a sense of urgency among the Admiralty. Standard prototype and testing protocols were eliminated and the gun was ordered into production from its preliminary drawings and proved to be remarkably accurate and durable in action. The gun weighed 112 tonnes with a barrel length of 52½ft. Its shipboard mountings were consistently in twin turrets and, following the Battle of Jutland, this Mk I mounting was modified to a Mk II configuration that increased elevation and maximum range. The most famous Royal Navy warship of the interwar period, the battlecruiser HMS *Hood*, incorporated the Mk II turret. World War One warships that were rebuilt and modernised for service in World War Two were equipped with another modified turret, designated the Mk I (N).

The BL 15-inch Mk I demonstrated its capabilities in action at the 1916 Battle of Jutland, reportedly scoring hits on German vessels from a record distance of 19,500 yards. During World War Two, the gun was credited with the longest distance shell strike between battleships as HMS *Warspite* scored against the Italian battleship *Giulio Cesare* from 26,400 yards during the Battle of Calabria on July 9, 1940. The big gun was also prominent during the bombardment of the French Fleet at Mers-el-Kebir on July 3, 1940, which prevented the Vichy government from handing over the ships to the Nazi Kriegsmarine. In the Mers-el-Kebir action, the French battleships *Dunkerque* and *Provence* were damaged and the battleship *Bretagne* was sunk.

A decade after the development of the BL 15-inch Mk I, the BL 16-inch Mk I was in development and, by 1927, production was underway at Armstrong Whitworth, Vickers, William Beardmore and Company and the Royal Gun Factory at Woolwich. The 16-inch gun was originally intended to arm the G3-class battlecruisers that were never built. Instead, it was reassigned to the two Nelson-class battleships, *Nelson* and *Rodney*. The guns weighed 108 tonnes with a barrel length of 60ft. They were mounted in triple turrets and placed forward on both battleships. The guns were considered less accurate than other available designs and actually prompted a re-focus on lower muzzle velocity 14-inch guns.

BL 15-inch & 16-inch Mk I	
Country of Origin	Great Britain
Calibre	15-inch (381mm); 16-inch (406mm)
Crew	70; 99
Range	33,550 yards; 39,780 yards
Rate of Fire	2 rounds per minute; 2 rounds per minute
Number manufactured	186; 29

380mm SK C/34

Bismarck and Tirpitz Firepower

Designed and built by the famed Krupp works of Essen, the German 380mm SK C/34 served as the main battery of one of the most famous ships of World War Two, the legendary *Bismarck*, as well as her sister ship, *Tirpitz*. Krupp undertook the design and testing of the big 15-inch gun in the mid-1930s and, by 1940, it had entered service with the Nazi Kriegsmarine.

Plans were made to up-gun the battlecruisers *Scharnhorst* and *Gneisenau* from their main 11-inch batteries, but these were interrupted by the exigencies of war. The *Scharnhorst* modification never got beyond the planning stages, while the *Gneisenau* project advanced with three new double turrets under construction by the early 1940s. However, *Gneisenau* sustained severe battle damage and the three turrets were reallocated to static coastal defence positions. Interestingly, during the pre-World War Two period of co-operation between the Soviet Union and Nazi Germany, the Soviets ordered 16 380mm SK C/34 guns,

with plans to mount them aboard the battlecruisers *Sevastopol* and *Kronstadt*, but these guns were never received.

The 380mm SK C/34 weighed 122 tonnes, with a barrel length of nearly 60ft, 5in. The guns were built with loose liner construction, including a tube with four rings shrunk along their length forward of the horizontal sliding block breech. The guns were mounted in twin turrets aboard *Bismarck* and *Tirpitz*, two forward and two aft for a total of eight. A shell from one of *Bismarck*'s main batteries denotated a powder magazine aboard the battlecruiser HMS *Hood* and sank the pride of the Royal Navy during the Battle of the Denmark Strait in May 1941. The new battleship HMS *Prince*

380mm SK C/34	
Country of Origin	Germany
Calibre	380mm (15-inch)
Crew	90
Range	38,896 yards
Rate of Fire	2-3 rounds per minute
Number manufactured	24

of Wales was damaged in the same engagement. *Bismarck* further had fired its weapons against shadowing Royal Navy cruisers and low-flying Fairey Swordfish torpedo planes to perhaps bring them down in the great plumes of water generating as the projectiles fell into the Atlantic.

Tirpitz was harassed throughout her wartime career and eventually sunk by RAF bombers. In the meantime, her guns were fired in the bombardment of Spitzbergen Island in 1943 and on other occasions. The 380mm SK C/34 guns were also used in coastal fortifications in Scandinavia and along the coast of France, where they fired from time to time across the Straits of Dover at targets in Britain.

TOP: This image of the battleship *Bismarck* underway reveals the size of its main 380mm SK C/34 guns. (CREATIVE COMMONS BUNDESARCHIV BILD VIA WIKIMEDIA COMMONS)

ABOVE: The 380mm guns aboard the battleship *Tirpitz* protrude across the deck as the ship is moored in a Norwegian fjord. (US NAVAL HISTORY AND HERITAGE COMMAND VIA WIKIMEDIA COMMONS)

LEFT: The forward main 380mm batteries of Bismarck are shown while the battleship rests in port. (CREATIVE COMMONS BUNDESARCHIV BILD VIA WIKIMEDIA COMMONS)

150mm SK C/28

Robust Secondary Armament

ABOVE: Both primary 15-inch and secondary 150mm armament are visible aboard the battleship *Bismarck* in a Norwegian fjord. (US NAVAL HISTORY AND HERITAGE COMMAND VIA WIKIMEDIA COMMONS)

RIGHT: This disabled 150mm SK C/28 is shown in a turret aboard the wreck of the pocket battleship *Graf Spee*. (US NAVY VIA WIKIMEDIA COMMONS)

Having most notably served as the secondary armament for capital ships of the Nazi Kriegsmarine during World War Two, the 150mm SK C/28 gun was also used in the coastal defence role by the Germans and in post-war Norway. The 150mm SK C/28 was designed by German arms manufacturer Rheinmetall beginning in 1930 and featured a vertical sliding wedge breech with barrel length of 25ft, 8in.

The weapon weighed around 20,000lb and was used aboard the famous battleships of the Deutschland-class, often referred to as pocket battleships. These ships included the *Graf Spee*, *Deutschland* (*Lützow*), and *Admiral Scheer*, which mounted the guns in eight single turrets to support their main 11-inch gun batteries. The 150mm weapons were used to engage lighter enemy warships, commerce vessels and aircraft. The guns were also placed aboard the battlecruisers *Scharnhorst* and *Gneisenau*, as well as the legendary battleships *Bismarck* and *Tirpitz*. They were planned for installation aboard the aircraft carrier *Graf Zeppelin*, but this project was cancelled.

Intended to augment the firepower of the major Krigesmarine warships, the 150mm SK C/28 was conceived as a lighter and more compact alternative to the earlier SK C/25 that equipped the Königsberg- and Leipzig-class cruisers constructed during the 1920s.

Design and testing were concluded by 1935 and the gun entered production as Germany re-armed publicly in repudiation of the Versailles Treaty. The SK C/28 was placed in both single and twin mounts with varied armour thickness depending on the particular class of warship being constructed. The turrets weighed up to 132 tonnes. Aboard *Scharnhorst* and *Gneisenau*, the guns were placed in four twin and four single turrets for a total complement of 12 guns, while *Bismarck* carried a dozen SK C/28 guns in twin turrets.

After *Gneisenau* was heavily damaged, her C/28s were dismantled and repurposed in coastal defence in Denmark and as railway guns. Those originally intended for *Graf Zeppelin* were moved to the coasts of Finland and Norway. One battery remained in service with the Norwegian armed forces until 1989. During World War Two, a total of 111 of the 150mm SK C/28 guns were eventually placed in coastal defence batteries.

RIGHT: This 150mm SK C/28 turret, once aboard *Gneisenau*, on display on the coast of Denmark. (WARTOURIST DANISH WIKIPEDIA VIA WIKIMEDIA COMMONS)

150mm SK C/28	
Country of Origin	Germany
Calibre	150mm (5.9-inch)
Crew	12
Range	25,000 yards
Rate of Fire	6-8 rounds per minute
Number manufactured	200 approximately

203mm SK C/34

Kriegsmarine Heavy Cruiser Weapon

The design and testing of the main armament for the Admiral Hipper-class of Nazi Kriegsmarine heavy cruisers was undertaken in 1934 by Krupp of Essen, Germany, and the gun entered service by the eve of World War Two in 1939.

The 203mm (8-inch) SK C/34 was one of the most powerful naval guns of its size deployed during the war and possessed outstanding range with its horizontal sliding block breech and barrel length of nearly 40ft. It also possessed an excellent rate of fire for a heavy weapon. Weighing nearly 23 tonnes, these weapons were involved in several well-known engagements during the war at sea.

The three cruisers of the Hipper-class included *Admiral Hipper*, *Blücher* and *Prinz Eugen*. *Hipper* was involved in several combat sorties against Allied forces and merchant shipping in the Battle of the Atlantic. Surviving combat, the cruiser was scuttled by its own crew in the harbour at Kiel after being heavily damaged by RAF bombers on May 3, 1945. *Hipper* is most famous for its encounter with the destroyer HMS *Glowworm* off the coast of Norway on April 8, 1940. *Hipper* fired her main guns at the diminutive destroyer, which rammed the German cruiser and sank as a result of the damage.

Blücher reached a rather ignominious end, sunk by torpedoes and heavy gunfire from Norwegian shore installations during the Nazi invasion of Norway on April 9, 1940. The ship was struck by two torpedoes and several hits from large 280mm guns. After catching fire, she sank with the loss of scores of seamen.

The 203mm SK C/34 guns aboard the heavy cruiser *Prinz Eugen* are best remembered for their role in the Battle of the Denmark Strait on May 24, 1941. While escorting the battleship *Bismarck*, *Prinz Eugen* engaged the

203mm SK C/34	
Country of Origin	Germany
Calibre	203mm (8-inch)
Crew	76
Range	36,608 yards
Rate of Fire	5 rounds per minute
Number manufactured	32+

Royal Navy battlecruiser HMS *Hood* and battleship HMS *Prince of Wales*. *Hood* was fatally struck by shells from *Bismarck* and *Prinz Eugen*, sinking with only three survivors while *Prince of Wales* was also damaged. *Prinz Eugen* was sunk during US atomic bomb tests post-war.

The Soviet Union purchased the heavy cruiser *Lützow* from Germany in 1940 before the ship was completed and commissioned it as the *Petropavlovsk* and later as *Tallin*. Eight SK C/34 guns originally intended to arm the cruiser *Seydlitz* were repurposed in coastal defences when the warship was not completed. Eight other SK C/34 guns were detailed to the German Army and deployed as the 203mm K railway gun.

ABOVE: The aft 203mm SK C/34 guns aboard the heavy cruiser *Prinz Eugen* at Kiel in 1941. (US NAVAL HISTORICAL CENTER VIA WIKIMEDIA COMMONS)

ABOVE LEFT: The barrels of the forward 203mm SK C/34 guns of the heavy cruiser *Admiral Hipper* are shown as HMS *Glowworm* crosses the German bow, April 8, 1940. (EUROPEAN UNION PUBLIC DOMAIN VIA WIKIMEDIA COMMONS)

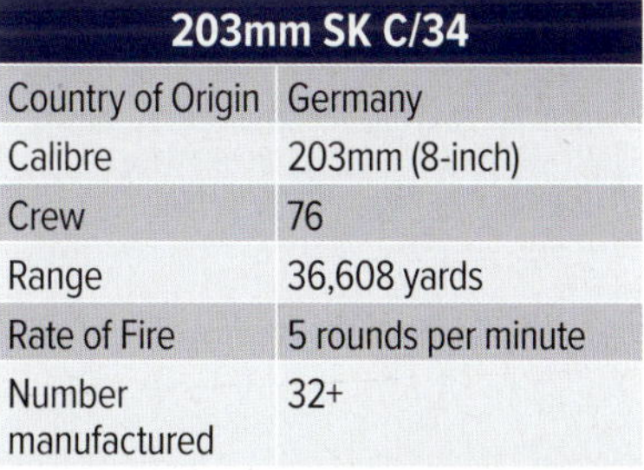

LEFT: Sailors crowd the deck of the German cruiser *Blücher*, on fire and sinking on April 9, 1940. (NATIONAL ARCHIVES OF NORWAY VIA WIKIMEDIA COMMONS)

BL 6-inch Mk XXIII

High Velocity for Royal Navy Light Cruisers

The London Cruiser Conference of 1929 – a co-operative effort between government and industry – resulted in the BL 6-inch MK XXIII naval gun, which armed several classes of Royal Navy light cruisers constructed from the 1930s through the end of World War Two.

The BL 6-inch MK XXIII was a high velocity weapon with improved mechanics that supplanted the earlier BL 8-inch Mk VIII, built under the terms of the Washington Naval Treaty. The Royal Gun Factory at Woolwich, Elswick and William Beardmore & Co built the new gun, which entered service in 1931 and equipped the Town-class, Fiji-class, Leander-class and Arethusa-class cruisers among other warships. The gun weighed nearly eight tonnes and its barrel length was 25ft. A key feature was the 'long trunk' ammunition hoist that was more efficient in bringing shells from magazine to breech than

earlier models and thus increased the rate of fire. Loading trays that were gravity assisted also contributed to an improved rate of fire, although the use of bagged ammunition propellant was somewhat antiquated, as were manual steps in the loading process.

Although originally intended for use in the anti-aircraft role, the BL 6-inch Mk XXIII proved adept in engaging surface targets. Its construction incorporated the Welin stepped interrupted screw breech block, which was hand operated with an Asbury mechanism. The barrel was built with wire wrapped around an A tube, the innermost cylinder of a built-up

BL 6-inch Mk XXIII	
Country of Origin	Great Britain
Calibre	6-inch (152mm)
Crew	60
Range	25,480 yards
Rate of Fire	6-8 rounds per minute
Number manufactured	469

gun, which proved reliable in combat when mounted in either twin or triple turrets.

The BL 6-inch Mk XXIII was widely used during World War Two. Perhaps its most famous engagement occurred during the 1939 Battle of the River Plate. When the Nazi pocket battleship *Admiral Graf Spee* was engaged off the coast of Uruguay near the capital city and port of Montevideo, the eight 6-inch guns aboard the cruisers HMS *Ajax* and HMNZS *Achilles* joined the 8-inch batteries aboard the York-class heavy cruiser *Exeter* in a fight with the main 11-inch batteries aboard the German commerce raider. After each side absorbed significant damage, *Graf Spee* turned for the harbour at Montevideo and was scuttled by her crew.

During the Battle of the River Plate, the 'Y' turret aboard *Achilles* is believed to have achieved a rate of fire of 10 rounds per minute before the crew became fatigued and firing dropped to six rounds per minute.

BL 8-inch Mk VIII

Britain's Heavy Cruiser Main Battery

The terms of the 1922 Washington Naval Treaty cast a long shadow across warship and naval gun construction during the inter-war years. Among its terms were the limitations of heavy cruisers to 10,000 tonnes displacement and maximum armament of 8-inch main batteries.

In response, the Royal Navy authorised the construction of the County-class heavy cruisers along with the BL 8-inch Mk VIII naval gun. The latter was developed in the mid-1920s and had entered service with the Royal Navy by 1927. It weighed more than 19 tonnes and was placed in twin turrets that weighed just over 207 tonnes. Its barrel stretched more than 33ft, and the gun operated with the Welin interrupted screw breech and Asbury firing mechanism. Primarily manufactured by Vickers and WG Armstrong Whitworth, the BL 8-inch Mk 8 was originally intended for high elevation anti-aircraft defence. However, its operation depended significantly on manual functions and was incapable of consistently tracking the improved aircraft of the era.

Early testing of the Mk VIII revealed the shortcomings of the turret mounts, including the training and elevation gear as being too slow for the anti-aircraft role. Further

BL 8-inch Mk VIII	
Country of Origin	Great Britain
Calibre	8-inch (203mm)
Crew	60
Range	29,920 yards
Rate of Fire	3-6 rounds per minute
Number manufactured	168

complications were found with the Mk I and Mk I* turrets that resulted in a re-engineered Mk II mounting by 1930, substantially correcting the elevation and gun training issues. While main batteries of the County-class cruisers were in four twin turrets, the two cruisers of the York-class were reduced to three twin turrets to save weight. One significant setback involved a misfire aboard the heavy cruiser HMS *Devonshire* in July 1929, which killed 18 men.

With the outbreak of World War Two, the Mk VIII gun went into action. During the Battle of the River Plate, HMS *Exeter* fired its main batteries against the German pocket battleship *Admiral Graf Spee*. During the *Bismarck* chase of May 1941, the cruisers HMS *Norfolk* and HMS *Suffolk* shadowed the great German battleship, *Norfolk* firing 527 rounds in one 90-minute period.

Later Royal Navy cruiser construction favoured the BL 6-inch Mk XXIII naval gun, which eclipsed further use of the Mk VIII. Six single mounts of the Mk VIII were located in coastal defence positions around Dover.

ABOVE: The 8-inch Mk VIII main batteries aboard HMS *Norfolk*. (COLLECTIONS OF THE IMPERIAL WAR MUSEUMS VIA WIKIMEDIA COMMONS)

LEFT: The forward 8-inch Mk VIII guns of the Australian heavy cruiser *Canberra* in port in 1930. (GOVERNMENT OF AUSTRALIA VIA WIKIMEDIA COMMONS)

BELOW: Damage to the 8-inch Mk VIII forward turrets aboard HMS *Exeter* after the Battle of the River Plate. (COLLECTIONS OF THE IMPERIAL WAR MUSEUMS VIA WIKIMEDIA COMMONS)

Type 36 45-calibre 14-inch

Standard Japanese Battleship Fare

ABOVE: The 14-inch guns aboard the battleship *Ise* point askew after the ship was sunk at Kure in 1945. (NAVAL HISTORY AND HERITAGE COMMAND VIA WIKIMEDIA COMMONS)

RIGHT: A 14-inch 45-calibre gun is installed aboard the battleship *Haruna* at Kobe in 1914. (GOVERNMENT OF JAPAN VIA WIKIMEDIA COMMONS)

RIGHT: The 14-inch main batteries of the battleship *Fuso*. (NAVAL HISTORY AND HERITAGE COMMAND VIA WIKIMEDIA COMMONS)

Type 36 45-calibre 14-inch	
Country of Origin	Great Britain
Calibre	45-calibre (14-inch)
Crew	98
Range	38,770 yards
Rate of Fire	2 rounds per minute
Number manufactured	100

(36 centimetres or 14 inches) when the Japanese converted measurements to the metric system.

After Vickers delivered a number of the guns, the Japanese took up production at the Kure Arsenal and Muroran factory of Japan Steel Works. The Type 36 was built from 1917. The Vickers-designed guns were installed aboard the Kongo-class battlecruisers, which also included *Kirishima*, *Haruna* and *Hiei*. Through the 1930s all four

were given extensive refittings and modernisation, resulting in their reclassification as battleships. The Type 36 gun weighed nearly 94 tonnes and its barrel was 52ft, 6in long. The gun was installed in twin turrets in the Kongo-class, as well as the later Fuso- and Ise-class battleships. Together, these warships comprised much of the Japanese navy's surface muscle during World War Two. They included the battleships *Fuso*, *Yamashiro*, *Ise* and *Hyuga*.

During World War Two, *Kongo* and *Haruna* shelled Henderson Field on Guadalcanal. Both *Hiei* and *Kirishima* were sunk in naval battles around the island. *Haruna* was sunk at anchor late in the war, while *Fuso* was blown up during the Battle of Surigao Strait. *Kongo* was sunk by torpedoes from the submarine USS *Sealion* in Formosa Strait on November 21, 1944.

During the early years of the 20th century, the Imperial Japanese Navy sought to emulate the most famous naval organisation in the world, the British Royal Navy. It did so in uniform and rank insignia, training and, most significantly, warship design. In fact, the Japanese contracted British shipbuilders to produce fighting ships.

Vickers undertook the construction of the battlecruiser *Kongo* for Japan in 1911 at its Barrow yard and consultation regarding the original design centred on the main armament. At first, the Japanese battlecruiser was to be armed with 12-inch main batteries. However, further discussion led to the adoption of a new 14-inch gun that was concurrently in development. Thus, the Type 36 45-calibre 14-inch naval gun traces its lineage to the original Vickers design presented to Japanese naval officers in the autumn of 1910.

When the Japanese opted for the 14-inch gun, its true calibre was concealed from the rest of the world with the label '12-inch Vickers Mk J'. The Japanese followed suit with their own 12-inch designation. Subsequently, Vickers disclosed the existence of the gun as being the 14-inch Mk A. The Japanese then produced subsequent models that were quite similar to the original, designating them the 41st and 43rd year types and then the Type 36

41/45 3rd Year Type

Modern Imperial Japanese Navy Weapon

The 41/45 3rd Year Type 16.1-inch naval gun was the first weapon of its kind designed and built entirely in Japan. Its name referred to its calibre and bore diameter, and it was similar to contemporary British heavy naval guns, except of lighter construction.

The 3rd Year Type weighed nearly 223,000lb and its barrel was well over 60ft long. The gun used the Welin interrupted screw breech block with an Elswick three-motion short-arm mechanism, similar to the British BL 18-inch Mk I naval gun that was in development about the same time. The 3rd Year Type was manufactured at the Japan Steel Works plant at Muroran on the home island of Hokkaido and the Kure Naval Arsenal. Intended to arm the Kaga-class battleships of the early 1920s, as well as the Kii and Amagi classes, it was mounted only aboard *Nagato* and its sister battleship *Mutsu* because the other classes were cancelled following the Washington Naval Treaty of 1922. On March 29, 1922, the gun was redesignated as the 40/45 3rd Year Type.

The Nagato-class battleships received the new guns during upgrades in the 1930s and other surplus 3rd Year Type guns were used as coastal defence weapons guarding the southern entrance to the Sea of Japan. *Mutsu* was destroyed by an internal explosion while moored at the Hashirajima fleet anchorage on June 8, 1943, while *Nagato* served as the flagship of the Imperial Japanese Navy on several occasions during World War Two. Most notably, during the early days of the war in the Pacific, *Nagato* was the flagship of Admiral Isoroku Yamamoto, commander of the Combined Fleet. *Nagato* survived the war and was turned over to the US Navy. It was finally sunk during post-war atomic bomb testing at Bikini Atoll.

The Japanese attempted to salvage guns from the wreckage of *Mutsu* during and after World War Two. However, these efforts were unsuccessful until a 1970 recovery effort that brought up two guns from its No 3 turret to display at the Museum of Maritime Science in Tokyo and the Yamato Museum at Kure.

41/45 3rd Year Type	
Country of Origin	Japan
Calibre	410mm (16.1-inch)
Crew	60
Range	42,000 yards
Rate of Fire	2 rounds per minute

LEFT: Battleships *Nagato* and *Mutsu* prior to World War Two during exercises involving their 3rd Year Type main batteries. (US NAVY NATIONAL MUSEUM OF NAVAL AVIATION VIA WIKIMEDIA COMMONS)

LEFT: One of the salvaged 3rd Year Type guns from the battleship *Mutsu* on display in the Museum of Maritime Science, Tokyo. (CREATIVE COMMONS 先従隈始 VIA WIKIMEDIA COMMONS)

BELOW: The battleship *Nagato* firing its 3rd Year Type guns at sea during exercises in 1936. (GOVERNMENT OF JAPAN VIA WIKIMEDIA COMMONS)

18.1-inch Type 94 Naval Rifle

Yamato and Musashi Might

ABOVE: Her massive Type 94 naval rifles clearly visible, *Yamato* undergoes sea trials in October 1941. (GOVERNMENT OF JAPAN VIA WIKIMEDIA COMMONS)

Built with wire wound construction, the Welin interrupted screw breech and massive barrels that were constructed in a three-stage process, the 18-inch Type 94 Naval Rifle was the largest weapon ever carried aboard a warship. Only the super battleships *Yamato* and *Musashi* mounted the huge guns, their true size disguised initially when their designation was listed as 400mm. In actuality the Type 94 was a 460mm gun, which weighed more than 162 tonnes. When mounted in triple turrets, the entire configuration weighed 2,510 tonnes. The barrels individually were nearly 68ft long. Both *Yamato* and *Musashi* carried nine Type 94s in three triple turrets.

The Type 94 was designed by engineer C Hada at the Kure Naval

18.1-inch Type 94 Naval Rifle	
Country of Origin	Japan
Calibre	460mm (18.1-inch)
Crew	200 at least
Range	45,760 yards
Rate of Fire	2 rounds per minute
Number manufactured	27

Arsenal in 1934, and construction was undertaken there. The entire theory behind the massive weapon was in keeping with overall Japanese naval strategy that dominated tactical operations throughout World War Two. The Japanese placed their confidence in being able to outgun and outfight any enemy in a single decisive surface engagement, and this concept was supported by the outcome of the Battle of Tsushima during the 1904-1905 Russo-Japanese War. That historic victory over the Russian Baltic Fleet seemed to validate the Japanese perspective, and *Yamato* and *Musashi* were the principle instruments of such a battle that would occur, they believed, with the US Navy.

In action, *Musashi* was sunk in the Sibuyan Sea during the October 1944 Battle of Leyte Gulf. A total of 17 US bombs and 19 torpedoes were thought to have struck the massive battleship, which had hardly fired its 18-inch guns other than in defence against the attacking aircraft. *Yamato*, on the other hand, was active during the Battle off Samar during the larger Leyte Gulf action in October 1944. Its big guns were reported to have scored hits that sank the destroyer USS *Johnston* and escort carrier USS *Gambier Bay*. *Yamato* was sunk during a one-way sortie against US forces fighting at Okinawa on April 7, 1945, again a victim of American aircraft.

RIGHT: The 18.1-inch Type 94 naval rifles aboard *Yamato* during the battleship's construction at Kure in 1941. (GOVERNMENT OF JAPAN VIA WIKIMEDIA COMMONS)

BELOW: The Type 94 naval rifles aboard *Musashi* firing during exercises in July 1942. (GOVERNMENT OF JAPAN VIA WIKIMEDIA COMMONS)

Granatenwerfer 69 210mm

Czech-built Heavy Mortar

When Nazi Germany occupied Czechoslovakia in March 1939, one of the trophies of its bloodless military and diplomatic coup was possession of the famed Skoda armament works. Skoda-built weapons were subsequently deployed to the German Army and served throughout World War Two.

Before the Germans arrived, Skoda had produced a prototype 220mm heavy mortar, an ideal weapon with plunging fire that could penetrate opposing concrete and steel fortifications. However, senior German officers did not pursue the continuing production of the heavy mortar for some time. When they did, a request was made to reduce the mortar to 210mm to make use of existing ammunition stockpiles. Skoda production of the revised weapon began in 1944 and the first of the units was delivered to the Wehrmacht by the end of that year.

The 210mm Granatenwerfer 69 weighed 6,173lb and its barrel length was nearly 10ft. The mortar had a maximum elevation 70° to deliver its plunging fire with ammunition ranging in weight from 187-240lbs depending on the type of target being engaged. Unlike many other siege-type weapons that required disassembly for transport, the Granatenwerfer 69 was built for movement in a single structure that could be towed behind tracked or wheeled vehicles. The base plate remained attached in transit and was situated above the tube. When deployed in firing position, the wheels were in specially designed shoes attached by rods to the baseplate and resting on a semicircular rail track. A rack and pinion system was used to raise and lower elevation and traverse was accomplished without having

to reposition the base with the installation of a balljoint that attached the baseplate to the mount.

Nicknamed 'Elefant' by its crews, the Granatenwerfer 69 developed a reputation for being hazardous to its own operators due to the use of sensitive contact fuses and the

loading procedure required. The mortar reached the front lines in limited numbers prior to the end of the war, but records indicate that it was in action on both the Eastern and Western fronts through the surrender of Germany in May 1945.

ABOVE: The Granatenwerfer 69 on display at the US Army Field Artillery Museum, Fort Sill, Oklahoma. (CREATIVE COMMONS STURMVOGEL 66 VIA WIKIMEDIA COMMONS)

Granatenwerfer 69 210mm	
Country of Origin	Czechoslovakia
Calibre	210mm (8.2-inch)
Crew	10
Range	6,890 yards
Rate of Fire	1 round per minute
Number manufactured	168

FAR LEFT: German soldiers operate a light mortar in the field, 1943. (CREATIVE COMMONS BUNDESARCHIV BILD VIA WIKIMEDIA COMMONS)

LEFT: Along with the heavy 210mm Granatenwerfer 69, Skoda also produced this 220mm siege howitzer for the German Army. (CREATIVE COMMONS BUNDESARCHIV BILD VIA WIKIMEDIA COMMONS)

Glossary

AA	Anti-aircraft
AFV	Armoured fighting vehicle
AP	Armour piercing
Battery	A tactical unit of artillery pieces of similar calibre and commonly grouped together
Breech	Closed end of an artillery barrel
Breech block	Apparatus for closing the breech of an artillery piece us a block rather than cylindrical bolt
Calibre	Inside diameter of a weapon's barrel
Carriage	Wheeled, tracked or static support for a mounted artillery piece that facilitates transport and fire positioning
Chamber	Section at the end of the barrel that receives and seats a projectile for firing
Crew	The soldiers or sailors required to operate an artillery piece during combat
Effective range	The greatest distance to which an artillery piece may be aimed with accuracy
Elevation	The firing angle of an artillery piece
Fire control	The technical process of aiming and delivering a projectile onto its target, particularly with automated assistance
Gun laying	Military term for aiming and preparing to fire a heavy weapon such as artillery
HE	High explosive
Muzzle	The front or open end of a weapon barrel
Ordnance	Military supplies, particularly weapons, ammunition and equipment required to sustain combat operations
Penetration	The degree to which a weapon's fired projectile is capable of compromising fully the integrity of a protected target
Range	The distance, usually measured as effective or maximum, which an artillery piece is capable of firing
Receiver	Mechanical section of an artillery piece that contains most of the weapon's working parts
Recoil	The responsive rearward energy created with the discharge of a weapon
Rifling	Grooves cut into a weapon barrel to cause spin and stabilise the projectile in flight
Screw	A breech-securing system that securely closes the back of an artillery gun tube
Shrapnel	Shell fragments generated from the detonation of an explosive round
Smoothbore	The barrel of an artillery piece that is not configured with grooved rifling
Trajectory	The arc path of an artillery projectile from discharge to impact
Tube	The main cylinder of an artillery barrel from which a projectile is fired
Turret	Open or enclosed housing that contains an artillery weapon

ABOVE: American troops prepare to advance with their wheeled 40mm Bofors anti-aircraft gun. (US ARMY SIGNAL CORPS VIA WIKIMEDIA COMMONS)

ABOVE RIGHT: German soldiers with a 50mm PaK 38 anti-tank gun mounted on a vehicle. (COLLECTIONS OF THE IMPERIAL WAR MUSEUMS VIA WIKIMEDIA COMMONS)

RIGHT: Soviet Red Army gunners training with their 76mm field artillery weapon in 1945. (CREATIVE COMMONS HANS SOOSAAR VIA WIKIMEDIA COMMONS)